7 Steps of Your Career Ladder

HOW TO CREATE YOUR OWN
SUCCESSFUL CAREER PATH
LIKE A CHAMPION!

Rodrigo S. Martineli

Caliente Press

Copyright 2017, 2022 by Rodrigo S. Martineli

ISBN 978-1-943702-52-7 (Print edition)
ISBN 978-1-943702-65-7 (Kindle edition)

All rights reserved. No part of this publication may be reproduced, distributed or transmitted in any form or by any means, including photocopying, recording, or other electronic or mechanical methods, without the prior written permission of the publisher, except in the case of brief quotations embodied in critical reviews and certain other noncommercial uses permitted by copyright law. For permission requests, write to the publisher, addressed "Attention: Permissions Coordinator," at the address below.

Caliente Press
1775 E. Palm Canyon Drive, Suite 110-198
Palm Springs, CA 92264
www.CalientePress.com
E: steven@calientepress.com

Ordering Information:
Quantity sales. Special discounts are available on quantity purchases by corporations, associations, and others. For details, contact Caliente Press at the email address above.

Original Front Cover Design: Ralph Cavero
Original Back Cover Design: Alexandre dos Santos
Revised Cover Design: Hector Castañeda
Book Layout ©2017 BookDesignTemplates.com

Contents

Foreword 1
Preface 7
Introduction 9
You 15
Qualities and Deficiencies 29
Your Current Job and Personal Criteria 43
North Star 55
Your Career Plan 71
SWOT 85
Differentiate Yourself 103
Pulling It All Together 115
Closing Thoughts 125
Afterword 129
Resources 135
    7 Career Essentials 135
    To-Do List Template 136
    Call-to-Action List 137
    More Resources 141
Acknowledgments 143
About the Author 145

Dedication

To Carolina.
My love, wife, mother of my kids.
I am so privileged to have you on my side.
Someone who has never ever left me alone.
Someone who I will love forever.
Thanks for supporting me, day and night!

People become really quite remarkable when they start thinking that they can do things. When they believe in themselves, they have the first secret of success.

John Wooden

Foreword

WHEN I FIRST MET RODRIGO MARTINELI, he was a very scared man. He had just left an incredibly successful career at Hewlett Packard Enterprise, and in the first two days of his very unexpected unemployment, he fell into reactive mode and immediately started a job as an Uber driver. When adding up all of the money he made in the first two days as an Uber driver after leaving HPE, he made almost exactly what he was making *in one hour* at the tech giant.

He did what any accomplished executive would do when confronted with an unanticipated situation— he swiftly reacted. But being in *reactive mode* vs. proactive mode brought him to a place where he was not moving forward with his career — he was actually moving backward!

As the founder of an executive career firm, I talk with top talent in some of the world's top-performing companies, and Rodrigo's story was very familiar to me. What was different about Rodrigo, though, was that most executives I speak with take about 2-4 weeks of convalescing after they've lost their jobs before they are mentally and emotionally prepared to then move forward with the next phase of their lives. Rodrigo, instead, called me a mere **two days** after he lost his job, and even though he was scared, he came to me very determined to move his career forward.

This was because he had, years ago, come up with the 7 steps to managing his life's work and knew what direction he wanted to go next. So even though he was faced with an unexpected hiccup in his career, he could regroup, reframe his objectives, and continue his trajectory toward his North Star, which you will learn how to do later in this book.

Another thing that impressed me about Martineli was his ability to execute and not just strategize. My firm helps multiple six-figure and seven-figure professionals, working closely with them to help land their perfect jobs and ensuring they get paid what they are worth. Therefore, I'm accustomed to working alongside extremely accomplished individuals with billions of dollars of responsibility, just like Martineli. I hear the stories of their accomplishments, and most of their accolades come from their strategies, but not on the actual personal execution of their objectives.

Instead, from the first day I met him, Rodrigo impressed me by his actions and not just his ideas. This is something you must know about this book — you must be ready to take action, *massive action*, to accomplish the goals you will set for yourself. In that respect, this book is different than any other career book you may read. The **7 Steps of Your Career Ladder** will take you on a journey to not only discover who you are and where you want to go, but also prepare you how to get there. This is so extremely important in today's job marketplace.

It might be helpful if I gave you some context of today's post-pandemic job market at any professional level. The job market has changed more in the last five years than in the previous 50 years combined. If it has been more than just a couple of years since you've actively looked for a job, it is important that you understand what the current economic picture looks like, as it has transformed how you must conduct an effective career search, whether you are qualified to make $50K a year or $500K a year.

Since recovering from the pandemic, the U.S. employment picture is at a tipping point never before seen in history. There is an average of 1.5 open positions for every unemployed person, and fully employed people are quitting at the rate of up to 4.5 million per month. This quit rate is *after* the Covid-19 lockdowns were eased. Even further unexpected, a recent number came out that shocked those of us in the career field – 51% of employed adults are looking for a different role. This overall workforce situation is dubbed *The Great Resignation.*

Even though there are plenty of open positions, we also see a perplexing timeline to find a new position. IN 2022, the average amount of time it takes to find a new job for those that are unemployed is 24 weeks.

This half year is a staggering number when considering that unemployed workers are heavily skewed at the lower end of the compensation spectrum. A good percentage of these people in between jobs are hourly earners, making $15 to $20 an hour. The more you are qualified to make, the longer it generally takes to land your next job. If you are seeking six figures, the average time it takes to land a role is 12 to 18 months. However, with the strategies outlined in this book, Martineli has given you the keys you need to find that perfect-fitting job in record time.

The online job boards only hold about 4% or 5% of all the jobs available in the market today...and yet 92% to 95% of job seekers use the job boards as their main form of looking for a job. Therefore, searching for a job online is so competitive that even with a Rock Star résumé, it is still highly unlikely that you'll get a positive response from the company.

In fact, about 80% of applications and resumes are weeded out through automation with Application Tracking Systems. An additional 80% of the ones that pass are eliminated manually by HR reps who often have less than five years of experience and do not intimately know how you personally would be a great solution to the challenges with which their company is currently dealing. Doing the math, this means that only a mere 6% of applicants for any job see the light of day. So, instead of facing the strong headwinds of these traditional hiring processes like everyone else is doing, the **7 Steps of Your Career Ladder** prepares you for the most effective ways to catapult your career forward.

These numbers above drive home the need for taking a dramatically different approach to searching for your next position, no matter what your current level of employment may be. What worked 10 or 15 years ago is no longer valid. The number one thing you must do to get a better paying and more personally fulfilling job fast is to stop doing what you have been doing presently and in the past. It's time to start over! The **7**

Steps of Your Career Ladder is the perfect book to start you on your path to success in your current career and every career you may have for the rest of your life.

One of the biggest advantages of taking the actions prescribed in this book is that, if you are ever confronted with a layoff or a sudden career change for any reason, there will be no gaps in determining what to do next. You will always know your path and how to walk it. No... RUN IT.

Tammy Kabell
Founder and CEO
Career Resume Consulting

Rodrigo S. Martineli

Preface

WHY NOT?

When I decided to write a book and "disclose" this process that took many years to develop and test globally, many people asked me, "why?"

I remember, during an interview on a Texan radio station, they asked me, "Why are you giving up all the secrets of this program in a book when you could sell it individually and make some serious money?"

It took me a split second to answer why. Because I wanted to enable hundreds, even thousands, of professionals just like you seeking a practical way to build a successful career plan. A plan that was not only doable but also with an actual dose of YOUR touch.

I knew that to reach this level, a book was the way. Also, I have learned something else with one of my mentees: 99% of professionals do not care about their careers. What they do care about is to be employed. So, if you bought or downloaded this book, congratulations. You are different! And being different at this moment in human history is critical.

Perhaps this is one of the core reasons for The Great Resignation. People have realized that they can have much more than just a job. They can pursue their dreams, their passions, and yes, they can get paid to do so!

After having more than 10,000 copies of this book sold and downloaded at Amazon, I have achieved one of my objectives: massify the distribution of this content.

This is now the second edition of **7 Steps of Your Career Ladder**. It is an updated, post-pandemic edition with minor edits and aligned with current market conditions.

The steps are all the same. And, now more than ever, they are helpful and essential.

The focus of these seven steps is precisely what people are seeking at this historic moment in time: a compass. Something that is not a one-size-fits-all outdated tome. And, it respects who you are and what you want (and why you want it – your North Star).

You may find thinking about and designing your career path challenging. Or perhaps you may not believe you can attain the results you want, even though others have. Toss those thoughts aside, as they are neither correct nor applicable to those who follow the strategies in this book.

The results will be yours. This is just the beginning. As you develop your career plan, and get to know yourself better, and gain an understanding of the seven steps, it will be time to act.

You have the power to pursue your career like a champion. And guess what? You just did the first step by diving into this book.

Go, enjoy the creation of your career path.

See you on the other side, champ!

Respectfully yours,

Rodrigo S. Martineli

Introduction

WHETHER YOU THINK YOU CAN OR THINK YOU CAN'T, YOU ARE RIGHT.
HENRY FORD

IN 2005 I WAS INTRODUCED to the managerial world.

Managing people is not an easy thing; helping them with their careers is even harder.

At the company where I used to work, we were "obligated" to have all our team members complete what is called an "IDP" or "Individual Development Plan." This was a guide, a template with questions that were supposed to help each employee create their personal career plan. But at the end of the day, that's not quite what it brought. Unfortunately, it actually created more confusion than help.

The IDP had questions such as: "What do you need to develop to achieve the next level?"

What? What is the next level? Which level are you?

Or even: "Where do you want to be in five years?" I don't know. I hope employed!

And worse, if you didn't know the answers, in the footer was written: "Talk to your manager."

So, if in the next five years I want to be a VP, my manager, who has been in the same role for the past ten years, can help guide me there? I think not!

I was very frustrated when my employees were coming and asking me questions on how to fill out this annual "career plan" form. Then, I decided I should do something to help them, in fact, something that would not only assist my team but also help me as a leader.

I had been discussing with my wife my frustrations with the company's so-called "career planning tool" for at least a couple of years. Then one day, she and I went to see a speaker to understand what a "high-impact training" was and how this kind of training could help us (she was having similar issues at her company).

During the speech, I clearly remember the speaker saying, "In order for you to know others better, you must better understand yourself." These words resonated. Deeply.

I was caught in a deep reflection process and both of us, my wife and I, started this journey. Destination: yourself.

After two "high-impact training" sessions and another dozen training programs related to human behavior, human behavior analysis, neuroscience, and other topics, I started to help people develop their careers.

The "7 Steps of Your Career Ladder" was born as an integrated program in 2009. It originally started with just five steps and, as everything gets improved over time and through usage, it became seven steps last year.

This program usually takes ten weeks to be completed due to the high degree of personal reflection required by participants. It is largely based on recent research in neuroscience, self-motivation, self-understanding, and other techniques.

My mission as a leader is to help bring this proven program to as many people as I can.

I have already helped people from different cultures, nations, religions, and even those speaking different languages to better identify satisfying career routes in order to be prepared and ready when career opportunities arise.

It doesn't matter your race, gender, age, or nationality: you need to develop your life and career to be successful. You cannot afford to allow either your life or your career to be determined by happenstance, accident, chance, or someone else's whim.

And that's what this book brings to you. A chance for you to take charge of your career, using a framework with seven insightful and reflective experiences to guide you into knowing yourself better and developing a solid career plan to achieve your definition of success.

Each chapter introduces a reflective exercise, sometimes combined with additional lessons and knowledge, and concludes with a Call-to-Action exercise.

It is critical for you to be extremely focused in reading this book, calmly and always performing the call-to-action exercises before moving to the next chapter. This is an important part of the process. You will shortchange yourself if you read through the entire book first and then go back to complete the individual exercises. So please do not do that.

Each experience triggers different stages of reflection and combined will certainly change not only the way you see your career, but also how you see your life. This is a life-altering book.

Previous Mentees
In this book, you will meet Robert, whose story illustrates how this process works. Robert is actually a combination of real stories that several of my mentees experienced while going through the process. I use Robert to bring these real-life examples to you, in order to make this process even more compelling.

The situations faced by Robert are a reflection of the process.

All successes and setbacks mentioned in this book are true too.

In every single process, we always need some reference to help us achieve better results, and Robert's story will certainly make you feel better connected to our proven 7-step process.

Previous mentees called this program "astonishing, transformative, essential, and personally enhancing," along with many other great adjectives. For their kind words, I am extremely thankful. For the successes they are experiencing in their own careers, I am both grateful and humbled.

Most of them realized how important it is to have a complete, solid career plan that reflects their personal desires and ambitions while simultaneously respecting their individual personal life choices. Also, these many mentees found, as you are about to, that once you have a useful career plan, if any hiccups — like an unexpected layoff — happen, you are much better prepared because you have control of your career decisions and destination.

Now, fasten your seat belt!

Destination: YOUR CAREER!

Enjoy!

CHAPTER 1

You

*ALWAYS BE YOURSELF, HAVE FAITH IN YOURSELF,
DO NOT GO OUT AND LOOK FOR A SUCCESSFUL
PERSONALITY AND DUPLICATE IT.*
BRUCE LEE

WHEN YOU WERE BORN, you immediately became a champion. In fact, science tells us you are a champion because among 40 million spermatozoids, just one reached the egg and nine months later you were born. How this sequence happened made you unique.

Your fingerprints, your DNA, and several other physical and biological elements make you unique. But that's not what we are talking about here. And don't worry, this is far from becoming a science or biology book and we will not continue discussing the science behind what makes you a unique individual. But there are some important scientific fundamentals to note about individual development and how this impacts your thinking and emotions.

From around three months inside your mom's womb, your brain starts developing synapses. Let me explain what this means for you.

At that time, you have only your brain and your central spine. Then inside your brain your neurons start to make connections. These connections are called synapses. Everything that is happening around you, believe it or not, is creating synapses. These synapses will reach 90% of your total connections around your first birthday and about 95-98% when you turn eight years old. This means that only 2% of your brain's synapses are created during the remainder of your life.

All these synapses make you unique.

All the connections your brain creates make you unique.

And why is this so important? If during the first 98% of connection creation a synapse is made and it means something negative, you will believe that negative thought until that particular synapse is exploded.

Yes, I mean exploded. The only way for you to disconnect a synapse is by literally breaking it. Then your neurons will make a new synapse.

All your experiences will create synapses.

All the synapses combined with your memory will create your personality.

Your personality is responsible for the way you perceive and interpret things. Your personality is also responsible for the decisions you make that impact your life and your career.

For instance, your moral values, mainly those that your parents taught you when they were raising you, play a key role, not only in your personality, but also in how you perceive things. And your perception is essential. In fact, perception is everything, more than reality. Every time you interpret something, it is 100% based on your perception, not reality. That is why it is so important you understand it.

Your moral values define your character and justify decisions during your life.

But, if somehow a bad moral value was set, you will carry that your entire life until an event comes along and breaks it (a bad moral value that was turned into a synapse). When that synapse is broken, you will be freed and start to see and perceive reality in a different way. Consequently, this will likely cause a big change in your life and perhaps even in your character.

Finally, here's an easy way to remember these scientific fundamentals: your brain is your hardware, your mind the software, synapses are like folders, empty ones ready to be filled once they connect, and your personality could be called the operating system. Like any computer operating system that can be upgraded, your personality can be improved, tweaked, and adjusted during the course of life.

Can you now see why it is so important you clearly understand what happens inside your head?

Step 1 — *Understanding You*

It is a conjunction of experiences, moral values, character, and personality that shapes your life, your decisions, and consequently your career.

You always have a choice.

You can always choose to take on a challenge, confront an issue, or simply change your direction. But the latter will not add value to your life and career. The latter choice is for ordinary people without career ambitions, and you are not such an ordinary person. Otherwise, you would not be reading a book on how to create a successful career path like a champion!

You want to understand how to climb the career ladder.

You want to go the extra mile.

You want success.

But first, you must know and understand your personality deeply. Because your personality directly impacts your career.

Once you realize how your personality plays an important role in your life, it is time to know more about it and understand it better.

Why?

Because, despite what you may have read or heard, it is important to understand that it does not matter if you are extroverted or introverted.

Today, living in the information era (some also say the exponential era), it is very common to see data flying around about how a person's personality influences their ability to grow and climb the corporate ladder.

It is also very common to see various infographics showing that extroverts, on average, are happier in their corporate jobs and that they comprise the majority in leadership roles (at least in the U.S.A.). But this does not mean you must be extroverted to win, to get a promotion, or even to ask for a raise.

There are now several studies and books which depict the various strengths that introverts bring to leadership and managerial functions.

However, for those who are introverted, most of the time those around that person do not know their aspirations, their preferences, and moreover, where they want to be several years from now in the organization. And that's where this can significantly impact a career.

Fundamentally, other people do not know what you want until you tell them. This means that it truly does not matter if you are introverted or extroverted. Others will only know exactly what you are thinking and what your career aspirations are when you tell them.

Since scientists have yet to create telepathy, you must tell others, particularly your managers and leaders, what you want career wise. However, if you do not yet know, that is also fine. We will talk about tackling this hurdle later in this book.

Whatever personality dimension a person has, balance is key. This means that for some situations in life (and career), introverts will need to speak up and articulate their career goals if these are to be achieved. Likewise, extroverts in some situations need to be quiet and focus on listening rather than talking. That's what I call balance.

Balance is key, the key!

Personality Traits

A key approach to studying personality types is by identifying and naming personality traits based on commonalities and differences.

I do not want to discuss personality tests here — although I have my preferences from ten years of coaching individuals on career choices. Instead, let me give you a quick overview of the most common personality traits that we can perceive in others. Maybe you will realize that you might have one or two of these traits as well:

Extroversion: normally people who are very talkative, social, friendly, and like to be surrounded by many people. They tend to deliver good performances on the stage or in presentations. The opposite is introversion, which can also be easily noted and recognized.

Neuroticism: people with high scores on neuroticism (based on a personality test) most likely experience anxiety, worry, fear, anger, and other sentiments that can lead to depression.

Perfectionism: those who do not accept anything but the great and perfect. This type of personality tends to spend a lot of time on what I call "cosmetics," such as changing fonts, colors, and shapes in a PowerPoint presentation several times. Back and forth and forth and back are common actions of those who are perfectionists. But remember: great is the enemy of good. In an era that runs faster than any era before, good is often both feasible and sufficient.

Agreeableness: empathetic and sympathetic people carry the agreeableness personality. This can be found in leaders who consider the opinions of their staff instead of only making unilateral decisions. Being sympathetic has a lot of benefits.

Impulsivity: it is perceived as a reaction without considering the consequences and is normally taken without a lot of reflection. Nowadays, many decisions taken by impulsive personalities can cause unintended results that sometimes are really bad.

In addition to understanding your personality traits, you also need to be aware of your personality characteristics.

For instance, being humble is a big characteristic. Everybody loves a person who is humble. Everybody loves a person who displays humbleness.

On the other hand, nobody likes an arrogant person.

However, if you are too humble all the time, you will certainly lose out on opportunities.

And if you are arrogant all the time, you will lose opportunities.

What if you stayed in the middle? Seek balance all the time and more opportunities will be available for you to evaluate and capture.

Being balanced will allow you to show your value without being arrogant and, at the same time, humbly show what you have accomplished.

Think about your career to date. Have you sometimes not bragged about your career successes because of your personality or because you just decided to be humble? In doing so, was a colleague promoted and not you?

You don't need to brag all the time, but you do not need to be quiet all the time either. Balance is the key.

You need to find the right moment to make your play. And that is critical for your success. It is critical for your future ability to climb the career ladder.

Of course, all the traits and or tests that you might use to describe a specific personality type are not necessary for you to understand yourself. My purpose here is to give you a short overview of personality traits that are very easy to diagnose and understand. You can decide if these are applicable for you. I strongly advise, however, that the discovery of your personality can bring several benefits, even the same benefits that happened to my client Robert.

Robert: A 7-Step Case Study Success
I met Robert (not his real name) a few years ago. During this first step of our unique Career Ladder process, we were discussing the results of his personality tests.

In fact, he was not strongly extroverted or introverted. He was placed very near the middle though slightly more on the introverted side. He was also very well organized but, unfortunately, he did not have high emotional intelligence scores.

I was asking some general questions about his results when he started to tell me that his co-worker, a very extroverted person, was bothering him.

"It's so difficult to see Mike take over all the leadership meetings and use these to brag about his results. He is undermining not only me but everyone on the team. This makes me so crazy that I feel angry and lose my thought process," he said about his co-worker.

I replied, "Look, we need to split things up here. We need to discuss three fundamental things: how you behave in the meeting, how to control your emotions, and what impact this coworker is having on your career opportunities.

"So, firstly, do you normally say something in this team meeting? Do you prepare yourself to position things you've done or ask questions that can help you keep the momentum of your good work?"

He said, "Well, I generally look at the agenda, and I sort of prepare myself for the topics. But I don't speak very often. I think talking about my own work should be discussed one-on-one with my boss, not in a team meeting."

I was observing his face as he spoke and noticed that he simply disliked what he had just described.

I continued to probe his feelings and perceptions.

"I don't want you to let your personality take over in this moment and minimize you, nor do I want you to change your personality. But before we keep going, let me ask you something, are there other executives attending the meeting other than your boss?"

"Yes, normally other executives get on the call or even participate personally in the room."

"Bingo!" I said. "That is why Mike is always taking over. He is not wrong, Robert. He is just taking advantage of this meeting to create a very important component of anyone's career: reputation. Reputation is key for your next job. Reputation can also be called your track record, but more interestingly, reputation can be just a good perception. And that is what you need to establish.

You need to deliver results, chime in, but not oversell yourself since this can be seen as arrogance. But you do need to showcase your efforts, results, and ideas. But remember, be careful. Bring something really compelling that can sound positive, impact the team, create good energy, or even something that can create benefits for your boss."

"I see," he replied.

"Now that we have discussed a better way for you to behave in the meeting, let's jump to the next factor: your emotions.

"Quick question: after the meeting is over, are you still angry with Mike?"

"Of course!" he replied. And once again, he looked into my eyes and said: "Here we go again!"

"No Robert, we are not going anywhere. You need to learn that situations like this are not beneficial for you. This is wasting energy, your energy. This is not creating anything good for you. In fact, it is draining your forces. Because your brain enters a loop and consequently you lose focus, your concentration declines, and this is really bad. The next meeting or activity right after this team meeting will have an unfocused and low energy Robert, and that's not good for either you or your company."

"Well, I understand, but this is bigger than me," Robert said, looking at me with scared eyes expecting the worse.

"I have an idea. Have you heard about strategic disengagement? You should add a small activity between this cumbersome team meeting and your next appointment. This will help your brain refocus and help you get back to reality while decreasing your anger. By the way, the strategic disengagement must always be used between two events."

"That's really interesting," Robert said and continued, "But what should I do?"

I said: "You can read an article, check your smartphone feeds, read some news, or even play a short mobile game. It must be something that takes you mentally away for a very short period of time, say three to four minutes. This helps you manage your brain better."

"I will do this next time and see how it goes. Thank you!"

"Hey, we did not finish yet. We need to talk about how Mike impacts you. Do you have any connection with Mike's activities?"

"No, he is in a different territory."

"So, why are you bothered by him?"

"Don't know well, umm...maybe because I heard some rumors that he might be the next boss and I want that role."

"Great, that's what I wanted to hear. Look, here is where your personality plays a key role: have you told your boss about your career aspirations? Have you indicated that you want to learn more and grow? But listen, to make that happen, you don't need only a good perception. You need results. Results will be transformed into credentials. And solid credentials create opportunities."

"OMG!" Robert said loudly, just realizing how important this conversation had become to his future career path. He continued: "Now I see. You want me to position myself to create a good perception that will turn into reputation and, combined with results, will show I have the credentials to have the job. That makes sense."

"Wait a minute, Robert, I did not say that this will guarantee the job. However, it will at least put you in the contest."

"I see," Robert replied with some reduced optimism. But before he started to go south, I continued with my advice to him.

"But to complete your readiness, we need much more than just to understand your personality. We need an insightful reflection into several factors of you to create the perfect map, not only for your next job assignment, but for your future, for your life, and for your career. Believe it or not, it's completely tied to your life. It's a big mistake for people to separate their lives from their careers. In the end, it's the same Robert, don't you think?"

He nodded to show his approval.

Then, I invited him to set the time for our next meeting to discuss Step 2.

And I was thrilled because I knew that Robert was going to be more alert to what he was doing. He would also be better prepared to present at the team meeting and to start paving a path that is required for any successful career: a path of results.

I was looking forward to the next step and learning more about Robert and his career aspirations. But at the same time, I was anxious to see the results of his reflection and actions. After all, as I explained to Robert, change is constant, and while progress may or may not happen, once change is happening with progress, personal breakthroughs are readily seen.

CHAPTER 2

Qualities and Deficiencies

*LIFE IS 10% WHAT HAPPENS TO ME AND
90% HOW I REACT TO IT.*
CHARLES SWINDOLL

IT WAS 11:45AM, one week following our last meeting and I was ready for my lunch with Robert.

For the last ten years, I have had the pleasure of mentoring many people across the globe about their career aspirations. The majority of these consultations took advantage of today's video-calling technologies. But Robert was lucky; we lived near each other and thus had the chance to meet face-to-face.

Even though he is a millennial, having made the cut by three years (they say that to be a millennial you have to be born between 1977 and 1995), I am pretty much old school and prefer *tête-à-tête* meetings over phone calls and video chats when working with my mentees.

I arrived punctually and, just before the time of our meeting, Robert arrived. We were about to start our session when he asked, "Before we start, can I share something with you?"

"Of course!" I replied. He seemed eager to get something off his chest.

He blurted out, "We are in a very difficult situation at home. My wife's company is in the headlines today. It seems that they will be acquired and she is concerned about her job. And so am I. In our house, our combined incomes are key!"

"Got it!" I said reassuringly, before starting to elaborate upon my answer.

"Robert, have you ever heard about a concept called the Circle of Influence?"

"Barely," he replied, "but how does it relate to our concerns?"

"Everything! Let me explain."

Firstly, I gave some context to him, saying that this was published in a book by Stephen Covey many years ago, the global bestseller *7 Habits of Highly Effective People*. I have used this concept both as a framework to be used in specific situations and as a method for thinking, sort of a unique angle to think about anything.

The Circle of Influence is a very focused way to look at situations, problems, and even opportunities. Basically, you place inside the circle the things you can execute or influence. Outside the circle are those things you cannot execute or influence. In the end, what is inside the circle are the only things you should worry about. Everything outside your circle of influence are things you cannot control; thus, you should never waste precious energy worrying about them.

I looked at Robert and said, "This means that you and your wife cannot impact or influence a decision about a possible acquisition of her company. Moreover, neither of you should be wasting energy getting concerned about it.

"However, if market signals or news reports begin to indicate a high probability of the takeover, there are several actions you could take."

With hopeful eyes, he looked at me and asked, "What can we do?"

"You can save more, adjust your expenses, postpone capital investments, or even change your investments to low-risk options. Your wife can even start looking around to see what other interesting job opportunities might be available for her. There will be a lot you can do to give yourselves peace of mind should the takeover actually happen. But wasting your time and energy wondering about what potentially can happen will not help at all."

In fact, this is a very common mistake we all make. We often waste time and energy thinking of things that can potentially impact us. That's not just you or me; it is everybody.

Do you do the same? Do you waste your energy thinking about things you cannot touch, modify, or influence? And, like most people, are your thoughts about the uncertainty of the future mostly focused on potential negative outcomes? If yes, let's learn how to stop doing this.

That's why I share the circle of influence concept as much as I can.

I have a quick exercise for you.

Anytime that you are seriously engaged in thinking about a big concern, get a piece of paper, draw a circle, and write reasons or actions inside and outside of this circle.

Believe me, this exercise will help you a lot.

Once you are done, start right away to execute all the actions inside the circle. Doing that will create massive results that can potentially impact the final outcome. After you execute all the actions, read the outside of the circle and acknowledge that you cannot change these. Realize this. And move on.

"That sounds very intriguing!" Robert said.

"Yes, it is, and when you use it, you will immediately experience the benefits. I hope you do it tonight and share this method with your wife. Pay it forward as well, and help more people think this way!

"Robert, did you bring the exercise with you?" I asked him.

"Yes, here it is!"

Step 2 — Qualities and Deficiencies
Have you ever thought that every single person has qualities and deficiencies?

I hope the answer is yes. Moreover, it is very interesting that most of the time, depending on your personality traits, experience, and other components, it can be difficult to list your own qualities and deficiencies. We simply see faults and positives in others that we do not see in ourselves.

For instance, sometimes people who are not open to new experiences can become very skeptical, perhaps even negative, and list more personal deficiencies than their qualities. As the saying goes, sometimes we are our harshest critics!

It is very common for people to list their deficiencies easier and faster than identifying their qualities.

If you stop right now and think about it, what would your two lists look like? Let's find out.

Pause your reading and list your personal qualities and deficiencies separately on two sheets of paper. Please note how much time you take on each one.

As you do this exercise, don't get bothered about quantities. You do not need to care if you list more on one sheet than the other. In truth, it does not really matter. The way you execute this exercise will reveal insightful information about you, such as your intelligence type. When you are finished, please return to read my analysis of Robert's own exercise.

When I looked at Robert's exercise, I saw five qualities and five deficiencies.

I made a brief stop, looked into his eyes, and said: "Do you realize you have a logical-mathematical style of intelligence Robert?"

"Why?" he replied with anxious eyes.

"You were looking for the same number of qualities and deficiencies, which shows your analytical IQ. Maybe this was unconscious, but I doubt it."

He looked at me again with a surprised face and explained.

"Well, I am a graduate engineer, so yes, I am a very logical and analytical person. But you knew that when we reviewed my résumé before we started this program."

I replied: "Yes, that's true. But while it is common for engineers to have a logical-mathematical predominant intelligence, that is not a rule. Usually, we have a combination of different intelligent types."

He was again surprised and I continued.

"Believe me, it is possible. Let me help you understand it."

Types of Intelligence
In 1983, Howard Gardener described the existence of nine different types of intelligence based on the enormous amount of research he conducted in this field:

Naturalist: focused on nature and living things.

Musical: focused on sounds.

Logical-Mathematical: quantifies things, searches for proof to confirm a hypothesis.

Existential: keeps asking about life and death.

Interpersonal: always senses people, feelings, and emotions.

Bodily-kinesthetic: master in body and mind coordination.

Linguistic: focuses on expressing ones' self by always using the right words.

Intra-personal: focused more on me and I than on WE.

Spatial: takes a 3D view of everything.

It is important for you to understand your type of intelligence. I really encourage you to take one of the many available tests to better understand your own intelligence profile. For one thing, this will certainly help explain why you make certain decisions and also how you behave in some situations. And, of course, how you describe yourself.

Also, as I described to Robert, we usually find that people have a combination of types of intelligence. It is rare for someone to fit 100% into only one of the nine types of intelligence profile categories created by Gardener.

I quickly went thru Robert's exercise and saw:

<u>Qualities</u>

Organized

Committed

Perfectionist

Works well under pressure

Loyal

<u>Deficiencies</u>

Lack of Confidence

Anxious

Introverted

Stubborn

Easily gets used to own comfort zone

Often, I like to start with an individual's qualities, but something triggered my attention this time.

I asked Robert how much time he spent on each side of the exercise, and his answer stunned me.

"I was done in probably 30 minutes with qualities and it took me almost two days to finish my deficiencies."

This was something different, completely unusual. As I noted before, because of all the things that condition our thinking, it is very common that we note our deficiencies faster than our qualities. But Robert was different. And I was thrilled.

"Robert, tell me more...why was this so hard?"

"I don't know. I actually tried to identify the deficiencies first, but somehow, I kept going to the quality side. So, I decided to stop and focus on qualities first, which was very interesting and somewhat fast. Then, I had to look for external opinions and talk with a few friends and even my wife."

I was truly thrilled because what Robert was describing to me was bigger than he was thinking. He had put aside his introverted nature and talked with others about what could be our biggest fear: how people judge us by our deficiencies...how they perceive the worst side of us...our flaws!

Even only talking with his wife and some close friends, that action revealed a lot to me.

Robert was listening and practicing the lessons. He was understanding that more important than trying to change his personality — which is never the case — he should adapt it in order to capture new information. This was a big step and it meant a lot.

I jumped right into the heart of his process: "What did your wife tell you?"

"Well, she said I am stubborn and get into my comfort zone so easily that sometimes I am blind."

"That's interesting, Robert. Let's talk more about that. Being stubborn is not always a bad thing. In fact, many would not even consider this a deficiency. We have some specific characteristics that I call the gray ones. Stubbornness, perfectionism, and commitment are examples of gray characteristics that I often explore with my mentees."

Some characteristics can be turned to the good or bad side quickly and that is why I classify them as gray ones. If you know which of your qualities and deficiencies are gray, you can potentially better manage these and turn them into advantages instead of allowing them to become disadvantages.

For instance, being stubborn can, in a good way, be a form of resilience.

Resilience is something that has a lot of value, both in the marketplace and in one's personal life. Resilient professionals are the ones who will overcome hurdles and obstacles to ensure that strategies are executed. Employers love to find those with this valuable characteristic.

On the other hand, of course, being stubborn simply because you want to get your viewpoint across, or you want things done your way, can really turn against you, again both professionally and personally.

Another example is perfectionism.

If you are a perfectionist in everything you do, it can be a problem. Some tasks have short deadlines — this sounds common to you, right? But if you extend the deadline because you want to achieve a perfect result, this may have negative consequences for the business and your work group. On the flip side, being a perfectionist brings higher levels of focus and focus is great.

Finally, commitment is great. But commitment, if misused, can be fatal. If you are committed to an organization, or to your boss, so strongly that you do not see the things happening around you, this can be a big pitfall. You may be so blindsided by your commitment that you fail to hear valid contrary advice being given to you by others.

As I said in the previous chapter, balance is key. Not just in your personality traits.

Balance is the key to everything.

Robert was listening to me with so much focus that I was extremely pleased. But I had to shift gears and make things a bit uncomfortable in order to drive home another learning point for him.

"Robert, I am so happy you put aside your pride and talked with people and nailed the exercise. However, I have a big concern here: why are people telling you that you easily go to your comfort zone? That is weird for me. Something is missing. I thought we were doing this coaching program to help you achieve the next step in your career and life. So, are you happy with your status quo?"

"Well, that's something that bothers me a lot, and you touched on this point in our last meeting. They say that it is because I do not share my aspirations, my desires, and what I want next. This creates a situation where everybody around me thinks I am stuck. Even worse, they think I liked my status quo. But this is not true. I want to change. That's why I came to you for career coaching in the first place."

We have all heard very famous speakers saying we have two ears and one mouth and that this supposedly is a signal for us to listen more than we speak. And that makes a great deal of sense.

Indeed, we should listen carefully to others. But we must also speak up, especially when it concerns our needs, wants, desires, and aspirations.

We must share our thoughts with others. Otherwise, they will not understand our hopes, dreams, and goals. They will also not understand where you are and what you are willing to do to grow professionally and personally.

Unfortunately, what we don't say is preconceived by others.

If you are not seeking progress, many around you will conclude that you are stuck or simply happy with your status quo and not interested in change or improvement.

That is why it is important to speak, to be heard!

"Robert, you shouldn't want just change; you should pursue progress. Change is a constant part of life and the work environment; progress is not."

"Yes, correct!" he replied.

"So, you took the first step by talking with people. Now take it further: share your ideas and desires. Start small, with your friends and family first. Then slowly increase the circle of those you speak with until you make it a habit to share your ideas and goals with others. People will then see you differently."

"OK, I will take this forward."

I continued to look at his exercise and turned things into a more comfortable conversation.

"Organized, loyal, and works well under pressure are pretty amazing attributes. These are critical qualities that every company is looking for. But be careful as loyalty can also be related to the comfort zone. So be careful with your qualities.

"Remember: nowadays, all companies hire based on hard skills (i.e., education, courses, track record, etc.) and fire due to soft skills (i.e., behavior, attitude, reactions, etc.). It is important that you police yourself not to allow your soft skills (or the lack of them) to get you in trouble or hold you back from potential advancement."

We were coming to the end of our session and Robert certainly was going through a deep reflection process. I was seeing evolution take place right in front of my eyes, happening instantly.

That is what should happen when you dedicate time and effort to find the most difficult answers to your questions.

This happens when you commit to knowing yourself better.

Progress.

The pursuit of progress should never stop. But you need first to start.

Call to Action
If you did not pause and do this exercise above, take two sheets of paper and write down your personal qualities and deficiencies.

Again, you do not care about quantities; put your focus on the quality of exercise. Take a look at how easy it is for you to create each list, as well as how much time you spend on qualities and deficiencies.

Once you have done this (or if you already did it above), ask your family members and close friends for their inputs on your two lists. This is a good way to improve how receptive you are to feedback.

After you collect all their inputs, spend 20-30 minutes each day for three to four days reflecting on what you wrote and what others have told you. Ask yourself: how can I maximize the use of my best qualities and what should I do about my deficiencies?

Remember that all-important gray area.

I guarantee you this exercise, combined with deep personal reflection, will be revealing for you.

CHAPTER 3

Your Current Job and Personal Criteria

*UNTIL YOU CHANGE THE WAY YOU LOOK AT THINGS,
THOSE THINGS WILL NEVER CHANGE.*
PAT RILEY

RIGHT BEFORE WE FINISHED our session, I gave Robert the instructions for the next step, as I usually do.

When I told him that we were going to talk about his current job, he had a predictable reaction.

"Oh, great! Finally, we are going to talk about my work and stop talking about me."

I briefly stopped, looked into his eyes, and continued.

"Yes, we are going to talk about your work and your current position. However, we will continue to talk about you since it's YOUR job, correct? Also, we need to review your personal criteria."

Now he was shocked. He was feeling lost again. Back to square one.

"What's wrong, Robert?" I asked.

"I don't know what you mean about personal criteria. Plus, what do you want to talk about regarding my current work?"

"Let me explain," I told him with a friendly smile.

Your Current Job

We are living in one of the fastest eras of human history.

Everything moves fast, seemingly almost at the speed of light.

Some people say that we are living in the abundance era, particularly an abundance of information. Others say we are living in the idea economy — you just need an idea to leverage the technical or technology resources to make it happen with less money than before — and, of course, strong and motivated discipline to execute.

I don't know exactly what era we are living in, but one thing I know: IT IS FAST.

And speed added to a "static" thing, such as time, creates a big problem, a modern disease: the "busy-ache."

Everybody suffers from "busy-ache."

Everybody is busy. So busy, in fact, that we cannot stop for a moment to review what is going on in our lives. What should ideally be a regular practice — pausing to reflect on our progress in life and in our careers — is now only a once-a-year or less frequent exercise.

Yet that is the reason we work: to have a comfortable and happy life, correct? How's your progress on this?

If you don't have time to review your life, what about reviewing your current job?

No, I am not talking about reviewing your work priorities, your project schedules, or the plans to achieve your objectives.

This review is about what is really going on.

What really makes you feel good or bad, content or anxious, optimistic or pessimistic?

Perhaps, what you think you need to change or improve.

Have you ever stopped to assess and evaluate your current job?

If you answered "yes," congratulations, though you are part of the minority.

If you answered "no," that's okay; now is the time!

Step 3 has three components:

What do you like about your current job?

What do you dislike about your current job?

What do you want to improve about your current job?

It looks very simple, right?

And admittedly, it does, at least at first glance. However, the lack of attention to these details creates a big problem. You don't truly know, within your heart, if you like or don't like your job (until you take the time to do some deep reflection on this). You have superficial feelings about your job and workplace, some of which you may express to others and some of which you keep to yourself.

Now, at this moment, you are probably thinking about your feelings toward your job, at least subconsciously, simply because I have raised the issue. And, you may also be judging this assumption and perhaps even thinking that I am completely wrong. But let me explain this a bit further.

Have you ever told someone that you were happy with your job even though you weren't?

Or, have you ever said that you were unhappy with your job but could not describe why? Even if you were actually happy?

Well, that is what I am talking about. We must have a solid perspective about such a critical component of our life: our work.

I will not even talk about how critical it is that you know about your career because that is why you are reading this book.

However, aside from gaining a better perspective about your job by listing what you like, dislike, and want to improve in your current job, doing so will also be revealing and priceless for those who want to pursue higher levels of success.

You may find it easy to list why you like your job. On the other hand, going beyond a few "tip of the iceberg" points may not be so easy.

Things such as good pay, a short commute to work, and many years at the same company are frequent responses we have seen. And, when we talk about what people tend to dislike in their jobs, the most frequent responses are things like the boss, the senior management, weak culture, and other non-tangible items.

But what truly makes you feel good or bad about your work?

Yes, that thing that you never told anyone. When you think about this, you will gain further insights into yourself.

What if you are unhappy in your job but reluctant to move on since the pay is good? I suggest you ask yourself, so what? Do you think you are capable of working in only one company forever?

Hey, let me tell you something: there is life and opportunities out there. Plenty.

So, be fearless and create your list. You may be surprised at your deeper feelings.

And don't forget to list what to improve. After all, even if you decide to remain where you are, you still want to see progress, right?

We don't want to be focused only on problems. We want to focus on solutions as well. And that's what matters.

Step 3 Session with Robert

This time Robert and I were meeting in a meeting room at his company.

I had arrived a few minutes before — punctuality is everything — and got comfortable in my chair when all of a sudden, he rushed into the room all excited.

We greeted ourselves as usual and he immediately initiated the conversation.

"This was the easiest exercise so far!"

I was somehow surprised and asked him why.

He said with some obvious glee: "It was about my job; it was easy."

We started reviewing the results. Robert was pretty much happy with his work location since his house was only five minutes away.

I started inquiring and challenging some of his mindsets, as reflected in his results.

"So, you like the commute but dislike the travel? Also, you like the company culture but dislike your boss, someone who has been working there for almost 20 years. Don't you think he is part of the company culture?"

Robert was stunned.

He looked over his list and started to think about how he could counter my inquiries and comments.

"Well, let's get started. Yes, I love the commute. It is pretty convenient. I can help my wife with the kids and sometimes can even go home for lunch. But I am traveling so much, every other week I am boarding a plane, and that is too much.

"Regarding my boss, yes, he has been working here for a long time, but his style is not compatible with the culture. We have a strong company culture and I don't see him surviving here."

"Robert, wait a minute! I recall we talked about your boss getting lined up for a promotion, and now you are telling me that he does not fit with the company's culture?

"Also, have you ever thought that if you are aspiring to take on his role, you might need to travel more often?"

Robert was once again stunned. Quiet. He was thinking about my words.

Those words touched him deeply. For a moment, he was lost.

I perceived he was entering into a reflection point and I wanted to keep going so he would have more to reflect upon.

"Robert, what about you complaining about overload and even about the company not respecting the employees by doing staff reductions over and over again? Don't you think this somehow impacts the culture?

"And why do you think stepping up and taking over your boss's role will make things easier for you?"

Robert took a deep breath and came back from his reflection journey. He started to realize how impactful this exercise was going to be.

In fact, this happens very often since we see the good and bad in our jobs and in our workplaces, but we rarely compare the two. We sort of treat these as salt and pepper. Two ingredients of our working lives that do not have trade-offs. And that's the problem. The obvious is not that obvious. We see the trees. A good coach helps us see the forest as well.

Robert started to speak.

"Yes, you are correct!"

I promptly interrupted him: "No, I am not and don't need to always be so. As your mentor, I am here to guide you, to help you navigate your career and life, to help you achieve the outcome you are pursuing."

He dropped his head down and continued.

"I mean, what you just told me is huge. Yes, you are correct, at least this time!" he replied, chuckling.

"Each factor on my list is not equal. Some are more important to me than others. So, it is very helpful that you challenge my assumptions. I was not comparing or contrasting the things I like with the ones I dislike. That was not obvious to me. Yes, I need to stop and think about how to look at my job more holistically. This list must make sense, both rationally and emotionally."

Great, Robert's reflection was moving him in the right direction.

He started to think differently. And that was my intention: make him change his mindset and evaluate all aspects of his current job situation.

The 7 Steps framework is built to help you think differently, reach decisions differently, and not give explicit answers. Robert certainly was learning a lot and progressing, which is the most important aspect of the 7 Steps process.

We quickly moved to the last part of the job x-ray and started to discuss some improvements Robert had listed.

The interesting angle of the improvements question is to — once again — change the mindset. After you list what you like and then dislike, it is time to build the solutions to fix the problems or perhaps the reasons why you dislike something in your job or workplace.

Our focus must be to quickly identify the issues and then invest quality time thinking about possible solutions. But frequently, we spend more time justifying our situations. This is a big mindset shift that we must make.

And it is critical for you to distinguish yourself as a problem solver.

Your reputation should be built on your ability to solve problems, not as one who proffers excuses or passes blame.

As Robert and I discussed the improvement opportunities he saw, the travel topic came back. Robert was suggesting less travel and more usage of communications technology.

I understood where he was coming from: he wanted to minimize his traveling time to be closer to his family, but who does not want that?

Moreover, for some specific roles, client-facing time is critical. This means that in some cases, if you don't like heavy travel requirements, perhaps you do not fit that particular role.

"Robert, be careful, there are some points that cannot be mixed into the improvements for your job simply because they are more convenient for you. Your travel preferences should be part of your personal criteria. Did you complete that?"

"Yes, I did. Shall we review?"

Personal Criteria
Your personal criteria should be the most important factors for you to be happy in your job.

The main components I usually see in this step are (but not limited to):

Location (or the ability to relocate).

Role extent: do you want a local, regional, national, or global role?

Leadership: do you want to have people reporting to you, or are you happy being an individual contributor?

Travel requirements: are you okay with some travel? If yes, how often? 25%, 50%, 75%? What makes a good work/life balance for you?

Commute time and/or the ability to work from home occasionally or regularly.

These are the common ones, but we can talk about many more. However, the essence of this exercise is for you to establish your personal criteria and your factors.

And guess what, you are probably thinking about them right now.

And I bet you didn't before.

Do you know why? Because we are all suffering busy-ache.

We are so busy that we don't have time to stop and truly consider our needs.

Unfortunately, we put our life and work on automatic mode and keep moving.

The collateral effect: bad decisions!

How many people do you know that have not changed jobs, even though they were completely unhappy? Or even destroyed their marriage? Or decreased their performance and ended up losing their "dream" job?

These situations happen because they do not have well-defined personal criteria for job and workplace happiness.

They did not evaluate that excessive travel requirements, or the client being in a 12-hour time zone difference, could potentially harm their health and family routines.

Yes, harm. And potentially irreversible harm.

Now, imagine if you took the time to think about your personal criteria.

The factors. Your factors and criteria.

They must be set. And there needs to be a thoughtful process for defining personal criteria.

This requires a great deal of effort and cannot be created overnight or in a few hours.

And in many cases, these factors cannot be fully defined only by you — you should discuss with your family what they think and get their input.

Before you look for another job, you must have your personal criteria fine-tuned.

That's the first thing. Not second. Not the last.

Otherwise, you will be running a massive risk of unhappiness, failure, or both.

Your "dream job" can be achieved, but remember, balance is key. What if you landed that big leadership title, with a big paycheck, and ended up alone or burned out? Would all the effort and sacrifices you made to achieve this be worth it? I suggest you pause now and put some real thought into this, and then continue reading this book.

Sometimes your "dream job" can become a real nightmare.

But, let me ask you something: where do you want to be when you think about retirement?

What is your career end-state?

Do you know?

Well, let's talk about it in our next step.

Call to Action

As described during this chapter, it is fundamental for you to undertake a solid assessment of your current job. On a piece of paper (or in an Excel spreadsheet), create three columns and start to identify what you like, dislike, and want to improve in your current job.

This is a great exercise that will help you build an insightful view of what you have.

Also, on another piece of paper, list your personal criteria.

Your results will be intriguing. And that's the purpose.

The power of reflection is starting to gain momentum.

CHAPTER 4

North Star

IF YOU'RE OFFERED A SEAT ON A ROCKET SHIP, DON'T ASK WHAT SEAT! JUST GET ON.
SHERYL SANDBERG

You have probably heard this before: "Don't regret the opportunities taken; regret the ones missed."

In fact, during your journey through the 7 Steps of Your Career Ladder, you learn more than just accepting the opportunities offered during your life and career. You also learn that taking control of your career path is crucial.

You know yourself better than you think. Especially now that you have worked through the first three steps of the Career Ladder program.

We all spend a significant amount of money on education throughout our entire lives, but most people do not spend much money or time to get inside and know themselves better.

You must understand your personality, your qualities, and even your deficiencies or weakness. You also must understand what you like and what motivates or drives you. And, you must have an x-ray vision of your current job situation for this can be the foundational step in determining a desirable and satisfying career path based on your personal criteria, preferences, and desires.

The first three steps of the journey have served as the basis for what's coming.

Now you need to:

Take control

Plan it

Implement it

My message to you is straigthforward: it is time to discover, build, and grow a successful career path.

But, if the majority of people just let their careers happen by circumstance, how can you take control and plan yours? And why should you? The answer to the latter is simple: because those who plan and take control of their careers are the ones who get ahead.

Do you want to climb a mountain?

What is the size of your mountain?

Do you want to reach the peak, or is halfway up fine for you?

Well, close your eyes and imagine the mountain you want to climb.

This mountain is your career. And what you need to figure out is how to climb it.

How to climb your own career ladder.

But, do you know where you want to reach?

Moreover, do you know your definition of success?

Is it the same thing? Perhaps.

Your career objective is your North Star.

The North Star Concept

Where do you want to be in your end-state?

No, I am not asking about your death.

I am asking where you want to be in your career when you say "I am done! I reached what I wanted!"

Where is that?

Where do you want to be in 10, 20, and 30 years? When you want to proudly acclaim: "I am ready to retire."

Maybe you think I am asking too many questions.

But here is why. I can guarantee all the answers are inside you.

Yes, right there.

You need to pursue something.

You must pursue your success.

People feel accomplished for many reasons. Your career is a reflection of big decisions in your life, such as college, specialization, post-graduation, MBA, executive education, etc. It is also a reflection of your personal decisions such as marriage, kids, travel, etc.

If all these big decisions are made and impact your career, why neglect the most important topic? That being your career journey.

Let me ask you again: What mountain do you want to climb?

Look around you. Every single person, friend, or relative has different objectives because they each have different success definitions.

Let me illustrate this through two typical stories that I often encounter. We will call these the John and Diana stories.

John is a 50-year-old executive. He has two boys, 15 and 16 years old, respectively.

John did not come from a wealthy family. He had to work hard to pay the mortgage, pay all the bills, and provide the best he could for his family. Guess what John's definition of success is? Having both kids in college. And once they graduate, he will pay off the house, work for a few more years, and then travel around the globe with his wife.

Diana is a 25-year-old sales executive in the healthcare field. She is saving money to have enough to get out from leasing an apartment and to making a down payment on her own house. She wants to be a homeowner and looks forward to paying a mortgage for the next 30 years. Diana knows John and she plans to be like him. To have enough money to send her future kids to college.

Do you see that the success definition differs on where you are in your life? Also, do you understand that this definition is situational? Here we have one person (John) whose definition of success is to pay off his mortgage. On the other hand, for Diana, the definition of success includes becoming a new homeowner and starting mortgage payments.

The same applies to successful career planning. Depending on your current situation, your definition of career success will be different from colleagues who are older, have a different marital status, or have a different family composition. However, no matter what your current status, you need to aim at something in order to have career progression success. And guess what: you must aim higher than simply your next career move!

Doing so will make you unlike most people, who just let things happen in their careers and consequently in their lives.

That's why you need to set your North Star. Those who are crystal clear about their definitions of success have a 50% higher rate of achieving their goals than those who do not have clearly defined goals.

Your North Star should be something very specific. But something that can (and will!) change over the years.

Moreover, your North Star is not dependent on your current position, title, or company.

Your North Star is part of your purpose, your mission.

It is something you must know. For, as the famous saying from the Alice in Wonderland story goes, "If you don't know where you are going, any road will get you there."

And it is a foundational rock of the 7 Steps method because everything after this step will be based on where you want to be.

Robert's North Star

Another week had passed since Robert and I last met. We were now at the halfway point of our 7-step program. This time Robert and I met in my brand-new office.

He sat in one of the comfy chairs and started to talk.

"I think you will not like today's session!" he told me bluntly. I asked him why and he continued.

"Until now, the program has been somewhat easy, but this step is too hard. I don't know what my North Star definition is. I don't know where I want to be in 30 years."

Robert is a 38-year-old executive and was concerned because he simply did not know where he wanted to be three decades in the future.

"Certainly, I want to be retired!" he stated.

"Robert, I understand. And guess what? You are not alone. 99% of my mentees in the last ten years could not define their respective North Star off the top of their heads. There is a lot of investigation and self-reflection required to extract this answer. The good news is that I will help you!"

Robert looked at me and I saw his eyes shining again. He was really concerned about his ability to keep moving forward in the program. But I was more concerned about the quality of this step. It is important never to rush this step of the process.

I gave Robert some examples of the questions he could ask himself to help him better understand the underlying desires he had for his career:

> Do you like your profession? Or do you want to shift your career into another field or another functionality?

> Do you want to go higher in your current organization? Considering your personal criteria for work/life balance, how would this impact that? Remember, with greater power comes greater

responsibility, and this also sometimes means greater time commitment as well.

What about beyond your next career move, that position that we discussed at the very beginning of this process? What would you like to be doing two or three moves after that? Assuming your next move is not going to be your final destination. [Note: this is a very important aspect to consider unless your next role is your final destination.]

He interrupted me and said, "No, it's not. I want more than the leader job we discussed previously."

"Yes!" I cheered. "That's what I want to hear. You are starting to get engaged in the thought process that I am looking for."

I continued: "So, if your boss is at the Director level, how higher do you want to be? Vice President? Senior Vice President? A C-suite executive?"

He looked at me and said: "I don't know. Sometimes I feel I would be happy with the VP title, even though I don't feel ready for that yet. Other times, I think I could evolve, be bold, and achieve a Senior Vice President role.

"I just don't know what my next move needs to be to put me on the path to getting me there."

"Robert, we are progressing, more than you realize. Let's split the conversation here. I don't want you to set your next career move. I want you to set your North Star. That means thinking (and then planning) 2-3 moves ahead. I want you to set your DREAM definition of SUCCESS."

"Wow!" reacted Robert.

"Now I am starting to understand...you want me to dream about it."

"Not exactly," I replied.

"I want you to tell me your aspirations, desires, and ambitions in the form of a title, a target that you will pursue. A target that will tailor what you are doing next and next and next again until you finally achieve it. Setting a long-term objective creates a different thought process. You will think differently about your actions and every single future career decision will be confronted with how it enhances your ability to achieve your ultimate target. Doing that will massively increase your chances to achieve it."

Robert finally understood the nature and depth of this exercise. And he realized I was giving him a path to help him through a deep reflection process to extract not only his definition of his North Star but also the reasons why this goal would be so important to his achieving satisfaction with his life.

We ended our session and he got back to his homework.

Discover. Build. Grow.

In fact, the situation Robert faced is very common. The large majority of people do not give themselves the chance to think deeply about their future, their ambitions, and how their career paths can be better planned and controlled. Too many people come to me complaining that they are super busy, suffering from busy-ache, and do not have the "chance" to set a career target.

Most, however, simply do not know where to begin. The Call-to-Action at the end of this chapter will help you alleviate this problem.

Also, another very common situation I see in clients, particularly those who are five to seven years into their working lives, is the tendency to set a low career path target. They typically think only of their next career move, or maybe two moves at maximum. This is a misunderstanding of setting a North Star goal.

Yes, it is important to focus on your short-term basic needs, such as a higher salary or the ability to buy a new car. But these short-term needs should be your temporary definition of success. Your North Star must be bigger than simply what you want to do next. It should be your ultimate success definition, even if you may decide to recalibrate it once or twice along your journey.

Robert Hits Another Road Block
After a week, Robert and I met again to check if he had finally found his answers.

Unfortunately, Robert was sad. Mike, the outspoken and somewhat arrogant co-worker, had been appointed as his new boss.

Robert was devastated.

How could they do this to him now? He was getting ready to take the role, but something happened and the leadership decided to immediately send his former boss to another role. And then, all of a sudden, and without warning, he had missed the opportunity to move into what he saw as his next role.

Robert started to complain. "I found my North Star, but now this will not happen anymore. I will need to wait until the next promotion cycle, or perhaps move away from my current company."

I looked at him and tried to calm him down.

"Robert, look, you've been such a great mentee. You are a hard worker and committed to this program. You dedicated hours to the exercises and, of course, this setback is tough. However, you must understand something. The way you think can dramatically change your results. For the good and even for the bad."

Think Positive
"Every time you are thinking about something, your brain is creating electric pulses and it doesn't matter if your thoughts are good or bad," I explained to him.

"Let's do a quick test: don't think about a red rose.

I bet you just saw a red rose inside your brain."

"Yes, that just happened!" Robert reacted.

I kept going. "This is what happens. Your brain just ignored the word 'don't,' and that's the problem.

"Let's try to change things right now. Instead of saying 'no' or 'I do not want to do this,' say that you want to do the opposite thing."

This will create a massive change because, instead of attracting bad things, you will start to attract good things. I am a true believer in energy, and when you create good energy, you are progressing.

"Let's begin the change now," I encouraged Robert, "and avoid as much as you can using the word 'no.' You will soon see the difference."

Robert was lost. Again.

He asked me, "I can try to think positive but now what's next?

"My North Star was dependent upon this promotion."

And before he could continue, I interrupted him and said, "Wrong! Your North Star is not dependent on your next-step promotion.

"Please share with me your North Star."

He was intimidated, but I had done this on purpose.

He handed his form to me. His North Star goal was written: SVP of Global Accounts.

I was thrilled. He was not happy because of his current situation at work, but he had achieved the goal of this step in the Career Ladder process.

Then I started to plant the seeds for his next step.

"Robert, firstly, well done. You did it. Now, let me tell you something. We will talk about your next move during Step 5, so do not get concerned about your career path being compromised because Mike was promoted and not you. You will learn that we have further options and we will explore all of them together."

With obvious relief, he was back to normal, even a little bit excited, then reacted: "Really?"

I said, "Yes! Your career path can be more unconventional than you can think. In fact, career paths are rarely as linear as we plan. They are usually circuitous in nature, twisting in various directions we may never expect. This is why it's important to have a North Star goal in mind, so you will know which unexpected opportunities to grasp and which ones to let go by.

"But I need you to focus on the lessons learned about the power of your brain. Also, I need to share with you one last thing. Let's talk about the three main rules of leadership. You will need to leverage these rules to increase your leadership reputation and build greater credibility with more people within the organization.

"You must take the lead, so let's start doing some leadership stuff."

Three Main Rules of Leadership

For most people aiming to move up the career ladder within their respective organizations, others must perceive and recognize them as a leader.

These three small tips will help you to change your behavior and accelerate the path to being recognized as a true leader.

Rule number one is: Listen with Empathy.

Everybody needs to pay attention to others, but it is very tough nowadays. We all have a lot of gadgets blurting out notifications from our phones, desktop computers, laptops, and tablets. Some even have watches and health bands buzzing all the time and taking our attention.

There is nothing worse than talking with somebody and not paying attention, especially for someone wanting to be perceived as a leader.

It is important for you to put yourself in the situation of the person that is talking to you. This creates a connection.

Listening with empathy will really make a difference when you are talking with somebody. Moreover, the other person will really value the time that you are taking to talk with them. Listening intently and with empathy is an important skill that starts the change to becoming recognized as a leader.

Rule number two is: Never Justify.

That's a big problem for most!

If we are late for a meeting, the first thing we look for is a justification to explain why we are late.

For example, you arrive late and you basically stop the meeting to tell people that the traffic was bad, or your daughter was sick, or your wife had a problem.

That's not okay.

Justifications don't change the situation, so why give justifications? Why waste your energy thinking about a good excuse?

Stopping justification dramatically changes how people perceive you.

If you change the way you are telling the message and recognize your mistakes, there is no reason to justify why you did it or why you didn't. Do that thing you were supposed to do. People will recognize the change in you. They will be impressed by seeing you take accountability and responsibility for your actions, rather than offering lame excuses or constantly laying blame on circumstances beyond your control. And that's what we want.

Finally, the third and last rule is: Always Suggest.

It is amazing how the construct of a phrase creates massive change for you to be recognized as a leader

Think about this. If every time you want something you position the desired actions to your team like this: "I want to go on this path." This will sound very commanding and authoritarian. We don't want to give others this impression. We want to show we are really working together as a team. This can be a very difficult habit to break. But if you want to work together, like a true team, it is a habit that must be broken.

Instead of saying "I want," you will be better off using phrases such as "maybe we could ..." or even "I suggest we do." Such slight changes in words and phrases can dramatically alter the perception workers have of their leader. And that's what we want.

This ability to focus on the leadership of the team, using team-building words and phrases, is critical for your career growth as a leader. Great leaders think in terms of "we" and "us," not in terms of "me" and "I."

As a leader, these three main rules of leadership will definitely help you to be recognized as a leader.

Recapitulating.

Rule number one: Listen with Empathy.

Isn't it bad when you are talking with somebody and the other person is not paying attention to you? Well, that is why it is important to display empathy with everyone you talk with.

Rule number two: Never Justify

Justifications will not change the situation, so don't waste your energy thinking about justifications or excuses.

Think about a plan.

Think about how you can change from now on to have a different result instead of justifications.

Use your energy to create, not to justify!

Rule number three: Always Suggest.

When you start to change your words from "I" to "we" and from "I want" to "would, could, or suggest," you will not only change your life but ultimately reach the goal of being recognized as a leader.

And that's what you want.

You are to be recognized as a leader!

I looked back at Robert once I finished my explanation of the Three Main Rules of Leadership and saw that he was excited but, at the same time, very puzzled.

He asked: "And how does this help me achieve my North Star?"

I replied: "Now that you 'lost' this particular succession cycle, we need to prepare you to grab the next opportunity that comes along. Even if the next opportunity that comes your way is not a vertical move, not Mike's new role, it can be somewhere else in the organization. And people need to recognize the great leader you are capable of being.

"So, cheer up and let's roll up our sleeves and start working on your next move. Step 5 in our Career Ladder process will provide the right framework for it."

Robert reacted well: "I am ready!"

Call to Action

Ask yourself: what is your North Star?

This question has proven to be very tough for my many mentees over the years. Admittedly, it is a difficult question to answer, particularly for those focused only on one rung of the career ladder. But it is key for you to have a target.

Once you have your North Star set, all your decisions will be made in alignment with your chosen destiny, making it more likely you will achieve your career goals.

Also, as you go further along in this book, the next steps will help you create your career path. Identifying and understanding your North Star is a fundamental part of this path's foundation.

So, where do you want to be in 10, 20, or 30 years?

What is your definition of personal and career success? How intertwined are the two?

What is your North Star? Why?

Which mountain do you want to climb?

Ready, set, go! Discover! Build! Grow!

CHAPTER 5

Your Career Plan

*A PERSON WHO NEVER MADE A MISTAKE
NEVER TRIED ANYTHING NEW.*
ALBERT EINSTEIN

YOU MAY BE ASKING yourself why we have waited until now to talk about one of the most important components of the career ladder: your career plan.

The reason is straightforward. What we have outlined so far in this book is a complete framework that provides a map for helping you to find your career path. And yes, the career plan is a big component, but it is not the only one. Or even the most important.

What is really important is combining all the components and integrating all seven steps together. This is why this book gives you an integrated framework. Each step contains another micro framework to help you build your career.

Therefore, the career plan is only one step among the seven steps approached by this book.

And here is my challenge for you: do you believe your career is not related to your life?

I truly believe that life has one side, career has another side, and both are two sides of the same coin.

Your career is more closely tied and linked to your life than you think and vice-versa.

If you take a job that starts to impact your personal life as soon as you begin it, this is the sort of issue that does not get better over time. Instead, it typically gets worse. This means one day you will need to make a big decision: either to move on to another job or to accept the losses it is creating in your personal life.

This is the kind of thing that has no right or wrong answer.

And guess what? Nobody can answer that question for you. This is why the previous step, finding your North Star, is important from both a career perspective and a personal life standpoint.

U.S.E. Career Plan

Do you have a career plan? And by that question, I truly mean do you have a complete career plan?

Yes, a real one. Written down, with everything, all the bells, and whistles, every single component.

Since you started this journey way back with Step One, the focus has been on your past and current situation. You have looked at your personal life and goals, your present job situation, and your current hopes, dreams, and desires for your future.

Now it is time to be forward focused, both short term and long term. And in doing so, you will start to think both big picture (i.e., 10+ years or more down the road) and specifically narrow down a little bit to your next career move.

Creating a career plan is not that simple. Do not be misled into thinking that this is as quick and easy as completing a template that your HR department has requested you to fill out listing your desires and aspirations. No, a career plan is everything that you have worked on so far in the exercises in this book, plus everything that will come along in the following chapters.

Creating a personal career plan is bigger, more complex, and demands much self-discovery, skills, attitude, and a commitment to execute. If it sounds like a big task, that's because it is. But the good news is that the hundreds of people who have used the 7 Steps of Your Career Ladder process will testify that this process is definitely worth the time and effort required.

Another very important thing that we must discuss is that we usually think there is only one way to climb the career ladder.

And this way is to move up. Constantly and frequently.

Get promoted. Take on more responsibility. Get a higher title.

Fortunately, this is not true. Almost no one has a successful career that is completely linear and only moves straight up the rungs of their career ladder. Plus, if it were true, anyone who has ever experienced a sideways or backward career move would get depressed and demotivated, thinking that their career hopes and desires had been permanently cut short.

We know better. This is why the 7 Steps for Your Career Ladder is not just another career plan. It is a unique tool and process to help you move forward in your career, no matter what short-term directions your career takes or what setbacks are encountered along the way.

We call this the U.S.E. Career Plan.

The U.S.E. Career Plan implements a different way of thinking about your next career moves.

This framework contains three options for you to get from where you are today to where you want to be in the future. Here are the three options:

1. (U) upward: it's the move up, your promotion, a vertical move. Taking over your boss's job or even a promotion in a different department within the same company.

2. (S) sideward: it's a side move, a horizontal one. It may be a role where you can expand your knowledge base or scope of experience, but it does not mean that you are promoted. This, however, does not mean that you are not growing, because knowledge and experience are likely required for your next subsequent move.

3. (E) external: it's your current market value. If you are laid off right now, what would you search for as your next job in the marketplace?

Robert and His Next Career Move

Robert was so excited. After working hard on defining his North Star, he thought he finally had something tangible to use to determine his next move.

To my surprise, the exercise was incomplete.

I looked at Robert and asked why he was only able to fill the Upward box in the template I had given him, leaving the Sideward and External boxes blank.

"Well, I have to say, this was a very hard exercise. I realized staying within my organization is closer to my reality, so it was really difficult to identify either a sideways move or an external one," he said.

"Robert, there is nothing wrong with that. I understand your situation perfectly."

Surprised, he said, "Really? Why?"

I explained: "Corporations must create a perception of longevity for their employees and the best way to retain talent is showing the promotion path. This means that one way or another, companies are conditioning you to think the next move is up. This is a false premise and leads to unnecessary competition between colleagues who are gunning for the same upward move.

In reality, for solid and sustainable career growth, you might need to go to another area within your organization to gain experience or credentials in order to step upward into a more senior role. Or even, equally as likely, you may need to move on from your current employer to develop capabilities required to conquer your North Star."

Robert quickly realized that everything I was saying made a lot of sense and was also highly pertinent to his current situation and his newly defined North Star.

"As a person who has developed your career so far at only one large corporation, you have a natural inclination to think that there is only one way to climb your personal career ladder. But that is simply not 100% true. Let's talk a little bit about the value of sideward and external moves."

Sideward Move
The size of the company or organization you are working for undoubtedly determines, to a large extent, your career path. But only if you allow this to be so. In fact, you must not allow this to drive your own personal career plan.

For example, if you work in a medium-sized company, by definition between 100 and 1000 employees, your options will not be as great as those found in a larger entity. In these types of companies, a senior manager will likely have, at most, two executive levels (say Director and Vice President) above them to aspire to. Or perhaps three if the manager wishes to become CEO one day.

Of course, your options in a medium-sized organization are larger than what may be found in smaller entities!

The concentration of functions is very high in such organizations, meaning that you would need different capabilities and experiences than you have today for you to become a Director.

And that is where a side career move can help you tremendously.

In fact, in either a medium-sized enterprise or a large company, a sideward move can be critical for your professional growth. Unfortunately, many professionals do not realize the importance and advantages of such a move. Some may actually see a sideward move as "being put out to pasture" or being "put in the bullpen for life." Those with this kind of attitude are likely to polish up their résumés and start looking outside the organization for their next career opportunities.

But astute professionals will take advantage of a sideways move to develop new skills, enlarge their internal and external professional networks, and learn about other parts of the company's business and operations.

Robert was listening to my explanation about the sideward moves when he interrupted me with this question: "Now that I understand better, what if my sideward move is to go to a completely different department? I always wanted to have a client-facing role but never had a chance."

"This is great, Robert!

"That's exactly where I want you to take your thought process. But, wait a minute, why have you never had a chance to work in a client-facing position?"

He replied: "Well, I never thought I was capable of developing the skills needed to have this role, but I think I could bring results."

"Interesting. Have you ever asked for feedback from the executives responsible for the client-facing team?"

"No, I've never thought it was appropriate to ask for such feedback. Why should I do this?"

"It seems we should talk a little more about the importance of feedback. Why don't we take a break, discuss that first, and then come back to talk about the values to be found in an external move?"

He relaxed and asked me to proceed.

Feedback

Feedback is one of the most important tools you should leverage in your career.

And guess what: it's free!

But be careful. You must be ready to ask, give, and receive feedback.

When we are asking for feedback, we must be ready for anything.

For instance, if you asked for feedback from your co-workers about how they perceive you and they answer that you are "arrogant," how would you react?

If the result of this process is negative, most likely this will bother you. But should it? Might it not be identifying a gap or behavior that you could remedy, thus making you a better person and colleague?

Naturally, we prefer to receive good adjectives about our skills, performance, and behavior. Likewise, it is natural to hate the bad ones, right?

But be careful. If some specific feedback is bothering you a lot, most likely, that "perception" of others is closer to reality than you really want. This means you should spend some reflection time thinking about why that feedback bothered you a lot. You should also look at the root causes creating the unwanted or undesirable perception.

Asking for feedback can be a tremendous tool for you to course correct your career, tasks, workplace relationships, and skill levels. But you must be ready to listen fully and thankfully, no matter what someone says to you.

You must be mature enough to understand that the feedback is not (or at least it shouldn't be) personal. It is a perception of another resulting from a particular situation, a series of events and interactions, or a personality trait that you are unaware of.

To be useful and beneficial, feedback must be both specific and timely.

For instance, if you have a poor performance in an executive meeting and I give you detailed feedback explaining the situation this can certainly help you.

However, if I just come to you and say that you were not prepared for the executive meeting or say it appears you were disorganized and unprepared, this lacks specificity. As a result, it does not help you and it may create more confusion than help in identifying areas where you can make improvements.

Robert was paying close attention to my overview of feedback, so I knew it was time to prompt him into action. I did this by asking him: "Are you ready to ask the executives what improvements or new skills are needed for you to be in a client-facing role? But, bear with me. You must be ready to listen to whatever they have to say."

"Yes, I am. Now I understand how important it is to ask for feedback."

"Robert, there is one more thing. When someone is giving feedback to you, be sure to ask questions related to what they tell you. Do not accept low context or vague responses that you cannot action. Asking questions will help you to identify if any gaps they mention are skills that you can learn or if they are caused by a personal trait or behavior you will need to modify. Get as much context as you can, as this will help move you forward."

Now that Robert was ready to seek feedback proactively, we went back to the exercise. He gladly filled the sideward box with the words Account Executive.

I was glad we were able to work together on this important part of the career planning exercise. We were now ready to discuss the external move option.

External Move
What if your company laid you off today?

What would be next? Yes, look for a new job. But, what job? Where? In which companies? In which industries?

Before you face the unwanted task of looking for new employment, it is good to know what your real value in the marketplace is.

Have you ever thought about this? Probably. Particularly if you parted ways with a corporation in the past. However, if you are currently still with your first employer, the answer is most likely "no."

Now, let me show you how to benefit from this situation. Let's assume you are employed and let's pretend that you are not happy with your current employer. So you decide to start a job search.

You are an Account Manager for a Services company. And you've been doing this work for almost two years. So, what is the job you start to look for?

Account Manager!

Well, maybe that's the wrong answer. Let me tell you why.

This particular job title is very ambiguous. For products-based companies, an Account Manager is a salesman. For a service-based company, an Account Manager is probably a client-facing role responsible for the client relationship in an end-to-end fashion. Do you see the difference? Job titles often have little in common across different industries and sectors.

Now, what if you have spent ten years as a project and program manager before taking this Account Manager job? What are your strengths that the market will value?

Yes, you have the PMP (Project Management Professional) and even the PgMP (Program Management Professional), both issued by the Project Management Institute. These certifications are important aspects of your credentials.

Is there anything wrong with pursuing a project management job? No, not at all. You may even find that a project management job has a higher status and more pay than an Account Manager position, especially with your experience and credentials. Just because the Account Manager job is a higher position in your current company does not mean this is the same in all companies or organizations.

That might be your true value to the market. In fact, you have more reputation, experience, and credentials to take this role, and these can be an important differentiator for the recruiter.

No, I am not saying that you should take a step back (if, in fact, this is a step back, and it well may not be), but if you lost your job, why not play in your sweet spot?

And this is why it is so important to have a career plan comprehending this move as well.

Since we rarely stop to reflect on our careers, imagine how rare it is to reflect on our true marketplace value? It is rare, but it is also fundamental to a good career plan. Think of it as a Plan B, so to speak.

Robert looked at me and said: "Are you tailoring this example specifically for me?"

I said, "No, what do you mean?"

He said: "Well, I had a very successful career as a Project Manager for five years, which was my 'ticket' to be in my current role. So, if I need to hit the market, this could be an option."

"Yes, this could be. But if you have a proven track record in your role as a business manager, you could pursue roles like this. The challenge is not to find the exact same titles, because from company to company the same titles might have different responsibilities."

"I got it," he said.

Robert filled the External box with Program Manager. Thus, after a solid 60 minutes of talking, exploring, and working together, we finally concluded Step 5.

Before we finished the session, I reminded him: "Now, go and ask for feedback on the client-facing positions and let's capture what is required for you to make your next career move to get you closer to your North Star. And remember, be ready to listen to whatever comes."

He agreed and we moved on. He had only the last two steps remaining to complete as he continued to move toward the initial conclusion of this journey.

Call to Action
As Robert just did, think about what would be your potential Upward, Sideward, and External career moves. Also, while Robert only listed one job for each of these, you may want to list two to three possibilities. At this point, the more options you identify, the better.

Remember that the easiest option, or the low-hanging fruit, is usually the upward move. That is because you feel comfortable in your current organization, and you have been programmed to think that only upward moves are smart moves. As we noted above, nothing could be further from the truth.

Now, go into reflection mode and identify what could be an optimal side move to utilize your competencies or create new credentials that would be required for a subsequent bold move.

And do not forget to identify the external options. If nothing else, this will help you know your true market value.

I understand how difficult this exercise can be, but this is a fundamental part of your career plan. Your future starts with the next step you make, so you want to start with a wide range of options to be prepared for whatever expected and unexpected opportunities come your way.

CHAPTER 6

SWOT

THE FUTURE DEPENDS ON WHAT YOU DO TODAY.
MAHATMA GANDHI

THE CURRENT JOB MARKETPLACE has become very challenging and demanding.

The demand for talent is no longer only about who the best is, but also who adapts best and fastest.

And when we realize how much information we must have to always be at the top of the chain, the challenge gets even bigger.

Once you extrapolate this to your life and career, staying up-to-date and handling this information load becomes an almost impossible task.

It is so difficult to manage the busy-ache, the last-minute demands, the inconsistency of the definition of urgent, and ultimately your own health. And, of course, all your family and other commitments you may have.

That's why it's so critical to do exactly what you are doing right now in meticulously going through each of the 7 Steps to Career Ladder Success.

Thus far, this book has given you wonderful tools to be easily adopted in your current situation and for identifying career aspirations. More than that, I hope the previous chapters have also taught you ways to think differently about situations that will possibly happen during your life and career.

So let me congratulate you. Why? The fact you are using these tools to reflect on your life and career is placing you at the very top of the market. Do you know why?

Because everyone is so busy with justifications, excuses, procrastination, and numerous low-priority activities that they just don't have time to travel inside this thinking process to find ways to improve their career paths and job opportunities.

That's why you have the advantage.

And this advantage comes not only through the practice and use of these tools, but also in identifying how to make them most relevant to your particular skill set.

An advantage can be equal to strength. But we must identify more than your strengths.

And that's what Step 6 of this process is all about.

It's a very famous tool, often used to evaluate businesses, initiatives, and projects.

But now, the evaluation is about to come.

Strengths, Weaknesses, Opportunities, and Threats

During every session, after reviewing the current step, I always take the time to explain to my mentees what the next step is.

Sometimes the explanation is easy. But sometimes, it must be very detailed in order to avoid rework and frustration.

In this particular step, details are very important.

Robert was happy because we were able to identify his U.S.E. plan. I started to explain that Step 6 was probably a tool somewhat familiar to him.

And probably it's familiar to you too. It's called the SWOT analysis tool.

In our next step of this career planning process, you are challenged to put yourself at the heart and center of a SWOT analysis.

So first, I need to clarify how I apply this tool to successful career planning. Strengths and Weaknesses are usually internal attributes in the business world, while Opportunities and Threats are external items, many of which the organization has no control over. So, the usual manner of using the SWOT tool is to have two sets of internal factors and two sets of external factors.

However, in applying the SWOT tool to our career planning process, we include Opportunities as an internal factor, thus giving us three internal factors to focus on and one external component.

Another very important point is that some Strengths can turn into Opportunities, as well as Weaknesses. That's why the depth of this exercise is huge. Using this tool, you can learn a lot about what is needed to execute your career plan.

In general, we can define these factors as:

Strengths: advantages against others, functional expertise, job experiences, and personal assets such as certifications, education, professional networks, personal resources, achievements, credentials, and values.

Weaknesses: tasks you avoid, areas where you lack confidence or where people think you are weak, functional skills and soft skills lacking that are needed for a higher position, and negative habits or even personality traits that negatively impact your career and life.

Opportunities: access to new people and knowledge, the competitive position of your company or you within the industry, new job opportunities for experiences (especially those which may provide an opportunity to fix a weakness or further develop a strength), temporary assignments, and cross-functional task forces.

Threats: obstacles that can create trouble for your job, causing your termination, unhealthy competition, technology shifts, industry shifts, economic recession, etc.

Lastly, we also include the way people perceive you as either Strengths or Weaknesses as appropriate.

Robert was with me and agreed that this would be a great exercise.

We agreed to the date and timing of our next session and Robert went back to his work.

The Big Surprise
This time 12 days had passed since our last session, and the insightful reflective experience in this stage created a lot of traction for Robert.

That was very pleasing as I was anxious to meet Robert and review his Step 6 homework. Over the years, I have found that roughly half of my mentees struggle mightily with this step, particularly in identifying weaknesses and threats.

This time Robert was different.

The handshake was firm and confident, just as we always talked about. But something else had happened. I could feel it.

Robert looked into my eyes and said excitedly: "Guess what?"

And I replied quizzically: "What? What happened?"

He continued: "Before I tell you, I want to thank you for always believing in me and my potential. This has helped me work through these steps and this process. I've learned a lot so far."

I interrupted him and said: "Is this a farewell?"

"No, of course not!"

I felt better and he continued.

"I was promoted. Now I am an Account Executive."

His happiness emotionally touched me as I knew how hard he had been working to attain a position like that.

He continued, "But I have to say that during Step 5, after we talked about how important it is to understand the options we have in our career, that was a big eye-opener for me. I went directly to the executives in another department and asked frankly about my chances. I thought it would not hurt to ask, right?

"And you won't believe what happened!

"They said there was an opening, and since I was an internal candidate, this could be an expedited process. I had a few interviews, and just yesterday, they informed me that I am officially moving to my new role."

Robert was astonished. But also excited and ecstatic. As well as a little nervous.

The fact that he went seeking the opportunity impressed me.

That is how we should be looking out for our careers — constantly and proactively keeping alert and attentive for new opportunities.

Opportunities can be created. Obviously, you can identify a potential opportunity, but if you don't have the right attitude, you might not "create" it. This is what Robert did when he decided to talk to the executives in the other department. While he did not "create" the account executive role, he did create the opportunity for him to be considered for that position by proactively engaging in a discussion. Prior to him seeking out those executives for a discussion, he was not even on their radar as a potential candidate.

I created many opportunities during my career by being proactive and staying alert to potential opportunities. During my corporate career, the biggest opportunity that I had opened up for me exactly the same way as Robert was now experiencing. I had approached the most senior executive and, with very constructive feedback, positioned my view about what could be improved within his operation. And, with a daring move, I asked him if I could be his chief of staff. His answer was no, but he had another opening that he offered to me.

It was nice to see history repeating itself, though this time for Robert.

I mentioned above that Robert was a little concerned about this transition and how fast he could adapt to this new challenge.

"Well, my first advice for you is to be laser focused," I told him. "And in addition to being resolutely focused on the most important issues your team is facing and the key results your new boss wants you to achieve, you must also know how to manage your energy and increase your productivity.

"Let's do this. Let's talk about the four secrets of peak productivity performance first, and then we will review your homework on Step 6, okay?"

4 Secrets of Peak Productivity Performance
Most professionals continuously seek ways to increase productivity to meet their objectives and deal with ever-increasing workloads and workplace demands.

In the past, the focus on productivity improvements centered on time management. However, this has evolved, and now we are talking about managing your energy, not just your time.

Basically, every day has 24 hours and allocating the time is not that hard because if you sleep eight and work nine, then you have around seven hours of "free time," right? (Unfortunately, for many, a good portion of this "free time" is spent commuting to and from work or being involved in work-related communications such as phone calls and emails.)

But what happens when you misuse your "work time," losing productivity?

Eventually, you will penalize your sleep hours, your lunch break, and probably even your family or personal time.

Also, if you are treating your health and fitness well, it is most likely that you wake up full, or nearly full of energy. Let's say your batteries are recharged at 100% when you leave for work and at night, when you are shutting down, you are probably close to 0%.

With that in mind, these four secrets will help you to increase your productivity in a way that your energy will be focused on what matters. This toolkit helps you to improve your efficiency toward reaching peak performance using the right levels of your energy.

Secret #1: Focus
Stop multitasking! Multitasking multiple activities and tasks results in poor quality and brain fatigue. This often results in energy wasted and time-consuming rework. The answer is: focus.

Being focused means that you are concentrating all your energy to complete the task at hand. And after you complete this task, a "magical" thing happens. It's called the "power of completion."

Completing a task in a "job well done" manner makes you feel so good it generates benefits for both your body and mind, making you feel ready for the next task.

But how to be focused in a world of notifications from smartphones, smartwatches, emails, phone calls, etc.?

The answer is your old friend, paper.

Personally, I have tried to use my email application to organize my to-do list, but realized that it was not working well.

Every time I was going to check my list, I ended up sneaking away to read a few email messages. And guess what? I constantly lost focus.

Creating a to-do list on paper every week and attending to these actions every day is a powerful process. I have developed a template for this which you can request via the instructions in the Resources Chapter later in this book.

By doing this, I am now completely focused on my priority actions and not on my incoming email messages. This has helped to increase my focus even more, resulting in faster task completion and enabling me to be more productive on a consistent basis.

I have learned the hard way how much distraction is created when my email keeps popping up all the time with notices and alerts. I have now turned the alert function off!

Secret #2: Strategic Disengagement

After you complete a task, your brain is "stuck" on the last action for some time, and it takes around 5 to 10 minutes to fully shift your focus to the next topic or meeting.

Strategically disengaging and clearing your mind for the next task will help you to re-focus faster.

How do you strategically disengage?

The main way to disengage is to execute quick tasks starting and ending in no more than three minutes, such as momentarily checking the Internet, reading some short articles or news, walking a little bit, or grabbing a fresh coffee. Even playing a short mobile game works very well.

Once you create this habit to disengage your brain, you will save energy and automatically increase your speed and readiness to focus on your next topic or activity, thus increasing your personal productivity.

By the way, this methodology also works wonders when you're working on a longer project or task. It's good to take a short mental break every 45-50 minutes to refresh your brain and stretch your muscles. Sitting too long working on a task is both mentally and physically taxing, and leads to faster energy depletion.

Experiment a little and find the ways that work best for you.

Secret #3: Plan a "Hard" Schedule

Use the calendar application on your computer or smartphone in your favor and not against you.

Doing a "hard" schedule planning — using recurrent appointments to consistently block time on your schedule —

will not only improve your time management but will also save your energy and help you focus on what's important.

Here's a list of some useful tips for planning your work schedule:

✓ Work hours: if you usually work from 8am to 5pm, set the work hours in your calendar. People should respect your calendar availability, although managing time zone differences can be a big challenge when working in a global enterprise.

✓ Transfers/Commuting slots: to the office and from the office – like 7-8am and 5-6pm. Why not tell everyone that you are in transit and are unavailable for calls or meetings?

✓ Lunch time slots: you have one hour to have lunch, right? Instead of using it for its intended purpose (to give you a mid-day break), why are you eating in just 20 minutes and then rushing back to work? Take your time, walk a little bit and get ready for the "second half" of the day. This will make a huge difference in the energy you have for the remainder of the day (both at work and in your post-work hours). And blocking this on your calendar will prevent people from scheduling meetings during your lunch time too.

✓ Email slots: create two to three 30-minute slots during the day for you to focus on reading and replying to emails. And, if you receive an email that requires some detailed effort, create a separate slot to focus on its execution.

✓ To-Do slots: create specific slots in your schedule for critical tasks such as follow-ups or to develop that executive presentation, etc.

Secret #4: Balance: Body, Mind, and Soul in Sync!
Balance is key.

Now, imagine how important balance is when you sync your body, mind, and soul.

The truth is: you must be healthy.

Let's see how to get there.

Water: Your body is 75% water and it is very important that you keep hydrating it. So, having a big bottle of water in your cubical, and refilling it at least twice a day, is the best practice. This helps you literally clear your mind and be energized for your tasks. Also, have a travel bottle that you can take anywhere. Why not drink water on the road?

Sleep: doctors recommend you should sleep at least seven hours a day. This is the minimum for most people to fully refill their energy levels. You do not want to wake up with less than 100% energy, right? So, sleep well.

Exercise: medical recommendations state we should exercise at least three times a week. So, don't postpone that walk, it helps you a lot. In fact, regular exercise creates more energy than it uses, so you are actually adding to your energy reserves through exercise.

Executing these tips well will give you a better environment for balance. Your body will be full of energy and doing the above will help your brain operate well. That is the key.

Back to Step 6
Robert was still processing these four secrets, their benefits, and how important it would be for him to adopt these productivity strategies right away in his new role when I asked him to show me his homework on Step 6, his SWOT.

Here is how Robert answered the Step 6:

Strengths
Very well organized
Committed
High emotional intelligence
Loyal

Weaknesses
Perfectionist
Anxious
Introverted
Stubborn
Not financially wise — unsure how to manage and report the financial numbers related to the customer account he would be handling

Opportunities
Increase confidence level
Get out of the comfort zone with a new job
Learn about sales

Improve client-facing skills

Threats

Economy downturn

Company bankruptcy

Spouse relocation

After I quickly looked at his personal SWOT analysis, I realized that Robert was indeed progressing very well through the program. His reflection process this time was almost at its peak.

As mentioned earlier, my mentees usually reach their reflection peaks between Step 5 and Step 7. And what does this mean?

Before I explain more about this, let me clarify something.

During the program, the mentee never knows exactly all the steps of the program. They are given each step one at a time, in sequence. The reason is our brains are very powerful.

If I tell you the steps and their sequence in advance, even if you swear to me that you will disregard this knowledge when going through the process, this is not possible.

Unconsciously, if you know the path you will be taking, you will damage the experience. Staying true to the process is critical, which is also why you cannot jump over a step (say go from Step 1 to Step 3), nor can you change the order of the sequence.

For instance, many people – and perhaps even you – ask why in Step 2 do we discuss qualities and deficiencies, and now in

Step 6 we do a personal SWOT analysis. Isn't this somewhat repetitive?

Well, that's the most amazing part of this time-tested program: the evolution of reflection skills and thinking processes for the practitioners going through the 7 Steps process.

Note that during Step 2, Robert included perfectionism in his qualities and lack of confidence as one of his deficiencies.

Now, after our previous reviews and discussions, when doing his SWOT with a completely different level of insightful reflection, he understands that perfectionism can be a weakness (as he and I discussed in our session on the importance of balance). He sees his lack of confidence as an opportunity for personal growth.

By realizing his qualities and deficiencies early in the process, then coming to know his North Star and next job, he now completely understands the need to develop different skills in order to further his career path. What was previously defined as a deficiency is now a great opportunity to learn a new skill or improve upon existing skills.

I talked earlier about perception.

The most important perception that we have is the one about ourselves.

If we are not self-aware about how we judge and perceive our emotions, we might be in trouble.

Once you see things from different perspectives and identify how these perspectives impact your thinking, dramatic changes happen in your life and consequently in your career.

Other skill improvement needs now appeared as well to Robert, such as the need to become financially savvy since he is now an Account Executive and will manage a client relationship for his company.

Also, some deficiencies solidify as weaknesses, such as being anxious and stubborn.

I looked back at Robert and asked: "Why did you include introverted as a weakness?"

"Well, I still think this is a problem! I still think I could improve on it!" he replied.

"Robert, we already spoke about this. One of the biggest pitfalls we have is to mix personality traits with situations. There is no problem, at all, for you to be introverted.

"You just need to communicate at the right time, with a solid position. Be heard, that's it.

"You do not need to over communicate. And to be introverted is not a weakness at all."

It seemed that this time Robert understood my point better, so I continued.

"By the way, if you did not talk with the executives, you would not be the newest account executive in your company, so you are far from being an *extreme* introvert."

He nodded his head, and eventually we closed this topic.

We moved to two other aspects of the exercise and I did like the way he had completed the analysis of threats and opportunities.

The fact that he turned deficiencies into opportunities and complemented this with some new areas in which he needed to grow now that he had been appointed to this new role was excellent.

I gave him feedback saying it was fundamental to learn from others how to be the best client-facing executive he could become. Moreover, that was a critical success factor in his new role.

We briefly touched upon the Threats. As Robert — and in fact none of us — have control of the economy or the companies we work for, those threats were well placed.

I also thought the fact that he added the spouse relocation as a potential Threat to his career plan was really well done and insightful. After all, an external factor that sometimes creates life changes for couples is when the one working spouse is asked to relocate for a new assignment. This is a topic that must be discussed and somehow planned for in both spouses' career path thinking, just in case it happens.

From a Step 6 "execution" perspective, Robert did a great job.

When we were about to finish our session, I looked at him and said: "Are you ready to define your brand? But not a simple brand. We need something real and solid. We need to define your distinction factor!"

Call to Action

Before going on to the next chapter, please grab a piece of paper, draw four boxes, and identify your strengths, weaknesses, opportunities, and threats.

This exercise helps you start to tie all the steps together to better identify a critical part of your career plan.

Take a moment away, step aside from your daily routine, put some concentrated effort into this, and really work hard on it.

You will be amazed how this small thing can be powerful and how much you've learned so far, not only about yourself but also about how to look at situations and events using different perspectives.

Also, be sure to go back and review the Qualities and Deficiencies lists you created in Step 2. Which qualities could be weaknesses if used inappropriately? Which deficiencies could be viewed as opportunities for learning new skills or fortifying existing ones?

CHAPTER 7

Differentiate Yourself

*THE HARDEST CHALLENGE IS TO BE YOURSELF
IN A WORLD WHERE EVERYONE IS TRYING
TO MAKE YOU BE SOMEBODY ELSE.*
E.E. CUMMINGS

I REMEMBER SOME YEARS ago, I started to hear and read about personal marketing, the importance of having a personal brand, and how to increase your value by creating and embodying a personal brand.

Many people bought books and, like flowers in springtime, personal marketing programs started blossoming all over the place.

At first, this was very positive since a lot of personal self-discovery was initiated. After all, for you to form your brand and do personal marketing you must know yourself better.

But later on, unfortunately, this turned into a very dangerous notion.

With more sophisticated techniques and marketing strategies, people started to "advertise" capabilities and create personas that simply didn't exist in reality and to which they could not live up to.

Many people were able to climb their career ladders using this technique, though with a significant lack of sustainability.

Unsustainable career growth is risky.

Usually, here is how I define the career ladder.

Once you start to work, you have ahead of you a wooden ladder.

Each step, obviously, is made of wood.

When you have just started your career, the ground is solid and, as you move ahead, you need to solidify each step. And each step on the ladder must be filled with concrete.

By doing that, you are growing in a sustainable way. And in case you fall off, you don't break the steps below on your career ladder, for they are solid concrete now.

On the other hand, we have witnessed many tragic situations where someone has been really good at personal marketing but created a not-so-true personal brand. This is not to say that these were totally fake or false, but it soon became clear that they certainly proclaimed an over-exaggeration of skills, competencies, and successes. In a very short period of time, we saw these people meteorically move up one or two steps in the organization. Unfortunately, by climbing their career ladders via this not-so-true personal branding method, the wooden steps were not being filled with concrete due to a lack of actual, solid skills and competencies.

Hence, when these folks fell, they definitely broke all the wooden steps of their respective career ladders and landed several rungs below (usually in a different organization) based on their true competencies and skills. Such dramatic falls were often bruising, both financially and to their egos.

Do you see it? That's not what I call sustainable growth.

Perhaps now you get why I compare wooden and concrete steps.

In sustainable career growth, each wooden step turns into a concrete step as you move up. So, if you happen to slip back, you will only fall one rung lower since that one, like all the others beneath it, is a concrete step.

But going back to the concept of a personal brand.

I am not against you having a brand. Not at all.

I am not against you undertaking personal marketing. You should.

I just want to help you to do so effectively.

Yes, you must have a personal brand.

A solid brand.

That properly positions you, transmitting your message, and differentiating you.

The job marketplace has evolved.

Dramatically.

The Internet has transformed the world of knowledge.

Studying in renowned universities and attaining certifications from upscale places like Harvard, Stanford, Oxford, etc., are no longer reserved only for those who can pay and attend these prestigious knowledge centers. You can now read and take classes basically from anywhere across the globe without being there.

Access to information and higher education is abundant.

And this has completely shifted how professionals are chosen for jobs.

Hard skills, such as those learned from universities, executive education, professional programs, certifications, etc., are important to create credentials (as we talked about before). So most likely, you will initially be hired for your hard skills.

However, career growth is usually a result of a person having acquired a combination of hard skills and soft skills.

Soft skills are critical.

Soft skills are things like leadership, behavior, emotional intelligence, motivation techniques, and many others.

And, most likely, you will be fired because of your soft skills.

But how do you differentiate yourself when the talent pool for higher-paid jobs comprises people with a great education, multiple language proficiency, and international experience?

It's a challenge.

All your differentiators are there.

Yes, there: Inside you!

Are you ready to learn how to extract these?

As usual, it demands deep reflection.

Robert and His Distinction Factor
This is Step 7.

The final one.

After ten weeks of intense reflection, this insightful experience program is coming to the end.

There is no way to say that I don't get emotionally tied to my mentees.

This 7-step experience changes their lives, and the level of knowledge I help them gain is usually pretty deep.

They get exposed to all aspects of their personal makeup and thought patterns, and I get to know them better than anyone but themselves.

For our last session, Robert arrived punctually.

He looked at me and said, "What's going on? Are you sad?"

"No, I am not. I am happy. Do you know why?

"Because I know this program changed your life and will continue to change it. But after all these weeks, I will miss our conversations. This process is amazing for both of us. You don't have any idea how much I learn with you guys."

Robert understood my point.

His final exercise was to identify how he could differentiate himself in the marketplace and within his current organization by creating a distinction factor.

The distinguishing factor is a combination of adjectives that together create a title.

This title is your brand, an expressive brand.

The first step is to list all the adjectives you think can differentiate you.

I recommend we have at least five adjectives.

You will need to mix and match them to create your title.

But be careful; not all adjectives work well here.

You must be picky and sometimes move away from being balanced and humble. In fact, it helps to be slightly arrogant.

You must understand what makes you better than others.

But not as a competition. As a tool that demonstrates what you are best at doing.

This is your value proposition.

Robert looked at me, and once again I saw his lost eyes.

"Well, perhaps we need to review my distinction factors," he stated.

"Why are you saying that?"

"You will understand in a bit."

I looked at his list, and here is what I found:

Organized

Committed

Self-starter

Resilient

Adaptable

Outspoken

Honest

Passionate

This was a great initial list, but some of the adjectives were not real differentiators.

"Robert, let's see. Do you really think that being organized differentiates you from others?"

He looked at me and said, "Maybe not."

"No, the answer is no. Even if you are not personally well organized, at least at work you need to be somewhat organized, so, this is not a differentiator."

"I would also question committed and honest as well. Being honest and committed to your job is a requirement, not a plus or a value that you bring that others do not."

He dropped his head down begrudgingly, for we had already cut three of his adjectives.

"Now, something very important is missing here," I added.

"We need to position you as somebody who wants to lead teams or someone who can have greater responsibility as an individual contributor.

"The word executive should be used when you do not have a need to lead people and can be happy being an individual contributor. It's very common, at higher levels, to have executives leading people and many people generalize the word executives as meaning senior leaders. But for our purposes, we are using executive to denote an individual contributor who does not have people leadership as a requirement for their job.

"And that's the missing link here. So, let me ask you a question. Are you a leader or an executive?

"That's okay if you cannot tell me now.

"Also, I did not find any adjective related to performance.

Here is what we are going to do. You will go back to your reflection process and try to answer these questions. Also, I need you to go a bit further to your arrogant side and capture what really makes you different from your peers and others. Think in terms of performance, execution, and whether it is better for you to be thought of as a leader or an executive."

Generally, Step 7 takes at least two weeks.

Robert acknowledged the need to work further on this step and return in a week.

There are some things that are hard to identify and definitely need an "extra push" to get out.

During the course of the 7 Steps, each person's individual reflection process develops (which is good as personal reflection is a critical soft skill that will serve you for many years to come). We also usually notice that this reflection skill gets accelerated after Step 4 and reaches a peak between Steps 6 and 7.

This development helps to find the most difficult answers.

Now, Robert needed this "extra push" to come up with some solid elements needed to create his distinction factor.

After another week had passed, Robert and I were ready to dive into his list. Here is what he brought this time:

Leader

Adaptable

Passionate

Outcome-oriented

Self-starter

I looked straight into his eyes and said: "Wonderful. Now we are talking. You made my job easy!"

He replied back, "Why?"

"Robert, you did such a great job. Now, it's time for us to create your distinction factor. Ready?"

I stood up and went to my whiteboard and started to play with the words.

I created five placeholders and was certain the last one would be the word leader.

We started to discuss the arrangement and, after a good 15 minutes of back and forth with these words being put into different placeholders, we came up with:

> Self-Starter, Adaptable, Outcome-focused, Passionate Leader.

He looked for the first time at his distinction factor and I promptly asked him: "Do you think this tells who Robert is?"

"Yes, absolutely yes!"

I was thrilled.

But for a moment, I saw that Robert was sort of lost again! I asked him what was going on.

He said: "Now that I know my distinction factor, what am I supposed to do? Tell everyone?"

I replied, "Yes and no. Your distinction factor is your business card. It's a way for you to present yourself, introducing your differentiators in a way to create intriguing opportunities to start a conversation or even make a second conversation happen!

"Also, you should start using your distinction factor in your professional social networks, as well in your personal social networks.

"As a brand, the more people knowing about it, the better perception you create. Remember, perception is..."

"Not reality," he promptly replied.

"Great, it seems that you captured the spirit of this program Robert. Well done!"

And that's exactly what we are supposed to do with our distinction factor.

After careful investigation and defining your distinction factor using five descriptive adjectives, you should use it accordingly to position yourself in the marketplace and within your current organization. But remember, your distinction factor must be solid.

It must be your real value proposition, not something fake or something that you do not recognize as a good description of you.

But before I let Robert go, I had to do one last thing.

I had to talk about Positive Attitude.

Positive Attitude

Have you heard this before: Attitude is a magnet. What you think is what you attract!

The way you approach anything in your life and career dictates the results.

If you approach life negatively, most likely, your results will be poor.

If you approach life positively, the trend for you will be positive.

I see!" said Robert.

"Are you telling me that if I am not strong enough on positioning my distinction factor, I will not communicate my message?"

"No, it's actually bigger than that!

"I am not talking only about your distinction factor.

"During every single step in this process, you have learned different ways to approach your career, your life, and most importantly, you learned to think differently.

"But all your efforts during this process, the self-discovery and the awareness created can just be thrown away if you do not approach your career, and everything else, with a positive attitude.

"You must understand that you have to do more than simply say I want a positive attitude. Everything that happens in your life has a resolution. The only thing that still does not have a remedy is death. Anything else has a solution.

"Now that you are going back to a new job position after this program, it is time to leverage the major change in your life. Have a positive attitude and you will see massive changes in your life!"

A little bit emotional, Robert thanked me for being supportive during the program. He promised that he would certainly continue to practice the lessons learned. And that he would also continue his reflection process to make sure he is fully aware of how he is conducting his career and reacting to anything that happens during his journey.

Call to Action
On a piece of paper, draw a big circle at the center and five smaller circles around it.

Think about adjectives that differentiate you from others.

Remember: common adjectives such as organized, committed, and honesty do not count since we are looking for unique characteristics and not common ones.

Also, please note the distinction between the words leader and executive.

The word leader should be used when you have advanced leadership skills and are pursuing a management role. The word executive is used to describe an individual contributor who has no people leadership responsibilities.

Once you spend considerable time with the outside circles, it will be time to combine and create your distinction factor within the inner circle.

Be careful how you market your distinction factor, but don't be afraid to publish it on your social networks and use it as your business card.

Your distinction factor is your value proposition!

CHAPTER 8

Pulling It All Together

YOU CAN'T CONNECT THE DOTS LOOKING FORWARD; YOU CAN ONLY CONNECT THEM LOOKING BACKWARDS. SO YOU HAVE TO TRUST THAT THE DOTS WILL SOMEHOW CONNECT IN YOUR FUTURE. YOU HAVE TO TRUST IN SOMETHING — YOUR GUT, DESTINY, LIFE, KARMA, WHATEVER. THIS APPROACH HAS NEVER LET ME DOWN, AND IT HAS MADE ALL THE DIFFERENCE IN MY LIFE.
STEVE JOBS

THE 7 STEPS JOURNEY has come to an end.

But this is not really the end. In fact, it is actually a new beginning.

Your new life and career have just begun.

If you have done the assignments throughout this book, this proven and well-established framework facilitated an introspective experience for you. Additionally, this 7-step process provided you with several techniques and perhaps even changed the way you will think about your career and life from now on.

And that was the objective.

Perhaps now you realize how important it is to take control of your career. Hopefully, this journey has helped you to structure your career plan completely tied with your life goals and desires.

Because, as I wrote before, life and career are two sides of the same coin.

The 7 Steps All Together

This journey utilized several techniques to help get you into a deep reflection process.

Firstly, we started with your personality – and you have additional personality tests listed in our resource section at the end of this book which you can use.

This step promoted the very first self-awareness exercise, but moreover, it also triggered the reflection process critical for the 7-step journey.

This provided insight into understanding your personality traits and how these impact your reactions to various situations.

It is so important to keep this in mind.

We often catch ourselves doing things or saying things we did not think we would do. This has nothing to do with your personality. It is completely situational.

We can be very calm but, if we face an extreme pressure situation, we could overreact and lose our temper.

The first step gave you an experience. The experience to really understand who you are independent of your current job situation.

And that is critical for your progress in your career, wouldn't you agree?

After we triggered this reflection, we discussed your qualities and deficiencies. And guess what? We were just going deeper inside you!

The journey to your ego (the word coming from Latin that means I) just started.

You needed to describe your qualities and deficiencies. Usually, my mentees can better describe their deficiencies than their qualities. Was this your experience?

A balance in this task can happen, but most people usually define their deficiencies better. At least in their first attempt at this exercise.

This second level promotes some real self-discovering facts that provide more fuel for your reflection process.

When you expand your thinking and realize that, instead of being only about your career, this book is actually about you and what makes you tick. Thus, in Step 2, you learned what a fabulous and important journey you were embarking upon.

We turned a little bit, and in Step 3, we talked about the x-ray process, where we discussed your current job and your personal criteria that defines a satisfying job for you.

Most people never write their personal criteria for job and career satisfaction. They sort of have an idea, but they never spend time thinking about the kind of job requirements and work environment that make the most sense for them.

Moreover, they don't think about what they like, dislike, or want to improve in their work unless somebody asks them.

Because we are too busy. We have a modern "disease" called busy-ache.

But, at the end of Step 3, you hopefully found it easier to talk about your job and define your personal criteria for job and career success.

In Step 4, the North Star concept appears. This is big and, like our sun, hard to look at without glasses and very difficult to face.

But your career North Star is truly like your personal sun. It is fundamental for your growth.

You must have something to pursue. Otherwise, when it's retirement time, what have you accomplished?

You invested a lot of time in Step 4 and finally defined your North Star.

Now you know what you are pursuing.

So, what's next?

It is like you are in the middle of two mountains and need to build a bridge.

The bridge starts with the next step, your next career move.

In Step 5, I presented you with the U.S.E. plan.

Yes, you might clearly know what is the Upward step — the desired promotion. But now you identified other perspectives as well. These were Sideward moves to complement your current skillset and the External move that looks at your true value proposition in the marketplace.

In Step 5, the reflection process is deep. This should have helped you to know more and understand better about both yourself and your career options.

From these highly valuable perspectives, the foundation of your career plan is built.

And this is where Step 6 comes in, using a common business tool called SWOT to describe YOUR strengths, weaknesses, opportunities, and threats.

The SWOT analysis comprehends not only the things you should capitalize upon and leverage but also those that you should either avoid or develop. It is also designed to identify the skills and capabilities that should be used as a foundation for your successful career.

And last but not least, who are you? How do you differentiate yourself from others?

Hey, you have something special. Something different and unique.

But what is this?

That is what you discovered in Step 7.

You must have a distinction factor. A true brand that shows how you are different from me, your friends, co-workers, relatives, and everybody else.

But not a simple "marketing brand" — marketers please don't get me wrong — but something solid. Real. The real deal! Something that defines you and to which you can live up to.

After these seven life-altering, deeply insightful reflection steps, you are finally "in charge."

You now have full control of your career, where you have been, who you are, where you want to be, and how special you are to be there.

And "to be there" means your definition of success!

Next Steps

I hope you followed the Introduction instructions and only moved to each subsequent chapter after completing a chapter's Call to Action.

As I wrote at the beginning of this chapter, finishing the seven steps is just the beginning.

Your sense of control is real now.

It doesn't matter what happens in your company. From now on, you have all the tools and information in place to make the best decisions for your career success.

The best decisions for YOU. Your career and your life!

Practice is the best way to absorb new ideas and turn things into a habit.

Even better is to pay it forward!

When we teach somebody, we are creating new paths.

Now that you understand the value of being the "boss" of your own career, talk with others about the importance of this for their own lives and successful careers.

You are in the driver's seat. Take people along for a ride!

Last Session with Robert

As he had been every time during this journey, Robert was punctual in arriving at the scheduled time at the coffee place where we had agreed to meet. However, he seemed different, somehow changed.

Clearly, this Robert was not the same person that started the program a couple of months ago. His outlook and demeanor came across as empowered. He looked and acted like someone who knew exactly what he wants and where he is going.

I start the conversation by telling him how privileged I felt to help him during this journey and the way I think he grew during this time.

He promptly agreed with me.

"Look, the level of discussion, reflection, and 'fight' inside my head has helped me not only understand better who I am but where I can be!

"If you did not believe in me and motivate me to talk with the other executives about my aspirations, I would not be in my new role.

"Sometimes, I feel everyone needs a person like you. Guiding and not only giving answers but also showing all the pros and cons of each angle.

"So, if you asked me to define this program with one word, I certainly would say: transformative."

"Wow!" I replied to him. "And why is this, Robert?"

"Because before starting this program, just being blunt, I really never cared about where my career was going. I always worked hard and had good jobs. But this program made me look at things differently. We must manage our careers the same way we manage everything in our life.

"Some people at the beginning said that this was a waste of money, and now they ask me what's happened."

"Robert, I completely understand. We spend a lot of money on our dreams, but we forget that our careers fulfill every single dream we have. Fortunately or unfortunately, that's the truth!"

"Yes, that's absolutely true!"

"But what else did you learn, Robert?"

"The seven steps program taught me some things about myself that are important to growing my career and to just making the most of life!

"I have a better understanding now of my strengths, of what matters most to me, and where I need to improve. But the program does more than just provide insight into those things right now. It teaches you valuable exercises that can be used again and again throughout your life as new things unfold."

"That's amazing, Robert!

"One of the biggest fears that I have is my mentees feel obligated to come to the sessions, to do the exercises, and that scares me a lot, so I try to do my best."

Robert replied, "Not at all. My sessions with you were the highlight of each week! In my busy life, I don't get a lot of opportunities to take time and focus on myself. But that's exactly what you helped me do, and that time is priceless.

"Your ability to help me by giving insightful guidance, understanding situations, encouraging me, and truly caring about my growth as an individual were key.

"I don't know if you realized, but sometimes we spent our sessions going through the 7 Steps exercises. But also, we just talked about challenges I'm facing or how to get through a stressful situation. No matter what we talked about, our sessions were always constructive and encouraging."

"Robert, these are very kind words! Thank you so much!" I must admit, this feedback had me grinning from ear to ear.

"Let me ask this then: what will you say to those who said you were wasting your time and money with this program?"

"That's a great question. I will tell them that I would recommend the 7 Steps program to anyone at any stage of their career. Whether you are just joining the workforce, actively looking for a change, or just wondering what's next for you, the 7 Steps program can provide invaluable insights. The program helps you to see more than just your end goal. It helps you understand yourself, so you can set your sights on something that i's right for you while making the most of where you are right now. It's about more than just career development. It's about personal development."

"Robert, that's outstanding. Now, what was the most important thing you've learned?"

Robert looked into my eyes and said, "It doesn't matter what the company is doing. I will always need to make decisions that are favorable to me, my career, and my life.

"If the company makes a decision to lay me off, or if I am impacted by any organizational change, I will not lose my head. I have learned how to take control and follow the plan!"

"Robert, I am so happy for you! I hope you keep pursuing your North Star success definition. And do not forget to review your exercises from time to time and practice these. It must become a habit."

I was so proud of Robert.

He had been thoroughly committed to going through the 7-step process since day one, and now he had finished the program with a completely different mindset.

CHAPTER 9

Closing Thoughts

*THE LADDER OF SUCCESS IS BEST CLIMBED
BY STEPPING ON THE RUNGS OF OPPORTUNITY.*
AYN RAND

SOME PEOPLE CAN HAVE very smooth careers, without much action or surprises.

Others can have careers resembling roller coaster rides.

And some can have very stressful careers, with terminations, layoffs, constant re-organizations, never-ending change, a revolving door of bosses, and other stress-inducing situations.

It doesn't matter which is your journey. The fact is that having a solid career plan makes all the difference.

The importance of taking control of your career is not fiction.

It's a true statement.

Once you compile everything we have discussed in this book and have your full career plan in place, I am sure you will be telling others to take control of their own careers.

And, most likely, you will wonder why you didn't make this journey before.

Mostly the answer will be inside you: because you did not think it was important.

For instance, nobody thinks about their value in the marketplace (as we discussed in the U.S.E. plan in Step 5) until they lose their job and need to search for a new one.

With a career plan, it's the same.

A career plan is like a GPS.

You don't need one until you realize you are lost.

And that can be too late.

I mean if you realize you are lost and need to look for a job, a very stressful situation is likely to happen.

One that can jeopardize your family. And ultimately, you!

Facts are here. The job market can be hot, but the candidates that will be hired are the ones better prepared. And that does not mean the ones coming only from the best schools. Remember, in the information age, companies are hiring based on hard skills and firing based on soft skills. A good career plan will help you identify and develop both your hard skills and your soft skills.

After all, balance is everything.

Please remember this.

Why You Should Take Control of Your Career

Have you ever realized that most professionals don't have a solid career plan and, instead just keep moving from one unplanned job to the next? (Do a mini-survey and ask people around you!)

On the other hand, the most successful people knew what they were pursuing quite well, and that was the number one reason they achieved the pinnacle of their career ladders.

We are living in the information age and the abundance of information readily available at our fingertips has created an enormous sense of urgency and tremendous speed.

The sense of urgency makes us busy, but it also makes us feel busier than we really are. That's what I call "busy-ache." The busy-ache prevents us from stopping and thinking about dozens (if not hundreds) of daily actions that impact our careers and lives.

Most of these actions divert us from our goals, simply because we are not aware enough of our goals.

And adding "light speed" to the marketplace obviously makes it faster, making each action you take critical since the job marketplace is a competition.

Those that know where they want to be have an enormous advantage.

Research says that just the fact of having an objective makes you 50% closer to attaining it.

But having a goal is not enough.

You must know yourself. And better than you think.

Plus, you must think differently.

And, more importantly, you must take control.

Once you take full control of your career by defining your objectives, you will become more acutely aware of your actions. And instead of being diverted from your goals, you will drive your actions towards these goals. The result will be that you perceive dramatic changes not only in your career but also in the other aspects of your life.

It's time for you to have your ultimate career plan.

Plan it.

Do it.

Climb the ladder.

Re-engage in the Process

All the Call-to-Action exercises are pulled together in the next chapter.

Also, we have a list of the career essentials distributed among the chapters for your reference.

From time to time, come back to the exercises, review your answers, and adjust your career plan as your life situation changes.

Re-read the essentials.

This is not a one-time static process.

It's the opposite: it's a live process.

This framework gave you several tools. Once you've done the exercises, you executed the framework.

The plan can be adjusted, refined, and tuned.

But never forget to update it.

It's your plan. It's your career. It's your life.

I hope you enjoyed the journey.

It's a pleasure to have you reading this book.

As I always say to the people I have worked with, let's keep pushing!

Afterword

Run to something, not away from something

HAVING KNOWN RODRIGO FOR SO MANY YEARS, it was an honor when he asked me to provide some additional thoughts and context to his professional story and career planning methodology. Simply put, when it comes to managing your career, running away from something is reactive and running to something is a conscious plan of action. I prefer, and recommend, the latter.

However, we all cannot create a 30 to 40-year career map when we start out in our twenties. So, the saying "have a plan" (let alone a conscious one) is definitely easier said than done. While you may not be able to create a specific plan with all of the details in terms of jobs, roles, companies, industries, locations, etc., you can start to define what is important to you, what makes you happy, and where can you make a difference. And in the end, always remember, you are in control. It is your life and you get to make the choices regarding your professional journey.

Let me share a bit of my professional story and the choices I have made over the last three and half decades. I chose to start my career in the aerospace industry because, at the time, I had recently graduated with an aerospace engineering degree. Seemed to make a lot of sense. However, I quickly realized the type of technical work I was doing was both unsatisfying and unrewarding.

Frankly, I determined that I was simply not a good engineer, nor was I making a positive difference for my team and company. Did I have a Plan B ready to go anticipating this challenge? No. However, I learned a great deal about what I did like to do, which was getting in front of customers, transforming business processes, and collaborating with a broad spectrum of people. It took some time to figure this out. In fact, it took several years. So, my first piece of advice is to be patient with yourself.

You need experiences under your belt to determine what you like and dislike professionally, but then you also need to act on those insights. Knowing what you like to do, but then having "implementation paralysis" to make a change, is a trap that many fall into. Our lives are too short to simply grind out our careers. Own it, drive it and live it through your choices. In essence, run to something.

So, I started to make some different career choices. Again, I would not characterize this as a "career plan," but, as Rodrigo discusses, it is about finding your North Star. Being close to customers, driving large-scale change, and leading people became my passion and my professional North Star. And with any journey, it is never a straight line. But the choices I began to make were always directionally aligned to my North Star.

As my career progressed, and my responsibilities grew, so did my focus on what made me happy. Now, it took decades for me to jump to a career model that simply focused on happiness, instead of role, responsibility, title, and compensation. But what I learned over the years is that happiness trumps everything else. Everyone has a different definition of happiness which is the way it should be. For me, I am a firm believer that combining happiness with one's natural skills and passion is a winning approach. Winning in this context quickly translates into good performance on the job, which leads to opportunities and future success.

After a decade or so in the aerospace industry, I transitioned into the IT services arena. This fast-paced, demanding environment really tested my North Star. In fact, I found my passion for clients, transformational change, and leading global teams to be a real joy. When I think about happiness in a professional sense, I remember a colleague of mine had a simple formula for his success. He stated, "you must enjoy the people you work with, the person you work for, and the type of work you do." I think this sums it up rather well.

Is every day better than the previous day? Not always. Do we all face ups and downs in our professional lives? Absolutely. However, it is our North Star that guides us through the day-to-day churn of our careers.

As time marched on, I found myself peaking in terms of my career happiness. So, what did I do? I took control. I made new choices. And I ran _to_ something, which has given me a new level of happiness, purpose in life, and a chance to make a broader impact. This brings me to the present day, where I am a full-time university professor. This opportunity not only allows me to give back to my alma mater, but also to teach the next generation of engineers about my lessons in career happiness and my equation for a successful and meaningful career. Another colleague refers to his happiness as what makes his "heart sing," which really resonates with me as well.

So, while we live in the times of the "Great Resignation," this is a time of taking control and leveraging your passions, your skills, and your dreams. Figure out what makes you tick, what skills you have, what roles are available to you, and how you can make a difference. Life can be overly complicated (especially one's professional life) unless we intentionally try to make it simple.

Now, go figure out your equation for success, determine your North Star, reach for happiness, and proactively *run to* the next opportunity with a "plan."

About the Afterword Author
Todd Taylor is a seasoned Fortune 50 business operations and transformation executive with over 31 years of corporate experience in the IT, manufacturing, aerospace, automotive, and financial services industries. He's now "back home," putting his experience to good use as a Professor at the University of Notre Dame, helping engineering students accelerate their future success.

Todd's passionate and client-centric leadership style exemplifies a visible role model of excellence by providing an active, hands-on approach to successfully leading a global enterprise. His experience includes $1B+ P&L ownership; 10,000+ multi-national team leadership; global account management; enterprise strategy development and execution; global contract management and negotiation; executive leadership training and development; CXO relationship management; and large-scale program and business operations management.

Todd holds a bachelor's of science degree in aerospace engineering from the University of Notre Dame and a Masters of Business Administration from City University of Seattle.

Previously he participated on the Industry Advisory Board for the College of Aerospace and Mechanical Engineering at the University of Notre Dame and was a Board Member for InTouch Credit Union. Todd also has many years of corporate diversity and inclusion leadership.

Resources

In this section, we share four sets of resources with you:
- The 7 Career Essentials discussed throughout the text
- My personal To-Do List template
- The Call-to-Action exercises for each of the seven steps
- Additional resources you can find through the 7 Steps Career Ladder website

7 Career Essentials

The 7 Career Essentials help you to take new and different perspectives about simple and complex situations, elevating your thought process so that you are always pursuing productivity improvement.

These 7 easy-to-adopt tips can help you have immediate results in your performance.

The essentials were spread across different chapters. Below you can see where you can find each one:
- Think Positive – Chapter 4
- 3 Main Rules of Leadership – Chapter 4
- 4 Secrets of Peak Productivity Performance – Chapter 6
- Circle of Influence – Chapter 2
- Reputation and Credentials – Chapter 1
- Feedback – Chapter 5
- Positive Attitude – Chapter 7

To-Do List Template

_'s Diary   Week of

Call / E-Mail	Actions		Delegate	Parking Lot
☐ 1	☐ 1	☐ 7		
☐ 2	☐ 2	☐ 8		
☐ 3	☐ 3	☐ 9		
☐ 4	☐ 4	☐ 10		
☐ 5	☐ 5	☐ 11		
☐ 6	☐ 6	☐ 12		
☐ 7	☐ 1			☐ 1
☐ 8	☐ 2			☐ 2
☐ 9	☐ 3			☐ 3
☐ 10	☐ 4			☐ 4
☐ 11	☐ 5			☐ 5
☐ 12	☐ 6			☐ 6

Note: This To-Do List Template can be downloaded through the Resource section at www.7stepscareerladder.com

Call-to-Action List

Step 1
Big Five Personality Test: www.outofservice.com/bigfive/
Isabel Briggs Myers' and Carl Jung's personality type theory: www.personalityperfect.com/test/free-personality-test/

Step 2
Take two sheets of paper and write down your personal qualities and deficiencies.

Again, you do not care about the quantities you put on either sheet. Place your focus on the quality of exercise.

Take a look at how easy it is for you to create each list, as well as how much time you spend listing qualities and deficiencies.

Once you have done this, ask your family members and close friends for their input on your two lists. This is a good way to improve how receptive you are to feedback.

After you collect all their inputs, spend 20-30 minutes each day for three to four days reflecting on what you wrote and what others have told you. Ask yourself: how can I maximize the use of my best qualities and what should I do about my deficiencies?

Remember that all-important gray area (see chapter two for an explanation). I guarantee you this exercise, combined with deep personal reflection, will be revealing for you.

Step 3
As described in chapter three, it is fundamental for you to undertake a solid assessment of your current job. On a piece of

paper (or in an Excel spreadsheet), create three columns and start to list what you like, dislike, and want to improve in your current job.

This is a great exercise that will help you to build an insightful view of what you have.

Also, on another piece of paper, list your personal criteria for job satisfaction. Your results will be intriguing. And that's the purpose. The power of reflection is starting to gain momentum.

Step 4
Ask yourself: what is your North Star?

This question has proven to be very tough for many of my mentees over the years.

Admittedly, it is a difficult question to be answered, particularly for those focused only on the next rung of their career ladder. But it is key for you to have a target.

Once you have your North Star set, all your decisions will be made in alignment with your chosen destiny, making it more likely you will achieve your career goals.

Also, as you go further along in this 7-step process, the next steps will help you create your career path. Identifying and understanding your North Star is a fundamental part of this path's foundation.

So, where do you want to be in 10, 20, or 30 years? What is your definition of personal and career success? How intertwined are the two? What is your North Star? Why? Which mountain do you want to climb?

Ready, set, go! Discover! Build! Grow!

Step 5

Think about what would be your potential Upward, Sideward, and External career moves. You should list two to three possibilities for each of these. At this point, the more options you identify, the better.

Remember that the easiest option, or the low-hanging fruit, is usually the upward move. That's because you feel comfortable in your current organization and you have been programmed to think that only upward moves are smart moves. As noted in chapter five, nothing could be further from the truth.

Now, go into reflection mode and identify what could be an optimal side move to utilize your competencies or to create new credentials that would be required for a subsequent bold move.

And do not forget to identify the external options. If nothing else, this will help you know your true market value.

I understand how difficult this exercise can be, but this is a fundamental part of your career plan. Your future starts with the next step you make, so you want to start with a wide range of options in order to be prepared for whatever opportunities, both expected and unexpected, come your way.

Step 6

Grab a piece of paper, draw four boxes, and identify your strengths, weaknesses, opportunities, and threats.

This exercise helps start to tie all the steps together to better identify a critical part of your career plan.

Take a moment away, step aside from your daily routine, put some focus into this, and really work hard on it.

You will be amazed how this small thing can be powerful and how much you've learned so far, not only about yourself but also how to look at situations using different perspectives.

Also, be sure to go back and review the Qualities and Deficiencies lists you created in Step 2. Which qualities could be weaknesses if used inappropriately? Which deficiencies could be viewed as opportunities for learning new skills or fortifying existing ones?

Step 7

On a piece of paper, draw a big circle at the center and five smaller circles around it. Think about adjectives that differentiate you from others.

Remember: common adjectives such as organized, committed, and honesty do not count since we are looking for unique characteristics and not common ones. Also, please note the definitions for the words leader and executive.

The word leader should be used when you have advanced leadership skills and are currently pursuing a management role. The word executive is used to describe an individual contributor who has no people leadership responsibilities.

Once you spend considerable time with the outside circles, it will be time to combine and create your distinction factor.

Be careful how you market it, but don't be afraid to publish it on your social networks and use it as your business card.

Your distinction factor is your value proposition!

More Resources

7 Steps of Your Career Ladder website:
www.7stepscareerladder.com

YouTube:
https://www.youtube.com/c/7StepsofYourCareerLadder

Twitter: www.twitter.com/careerladderbk

Instagram: www.instagram.com/careerladderbook/

Acknowledgments

To some, I was a good listener. To others, I was articulate and passionate.

It doesn't matter your choice of adjective for me. All of you that have crossed my path have taught me things that will be forever with me.

Here you are: Emerson Dipardo, Maria do Carmo Sanches, Albertino Gomes, Celio Bozola, Robson Ferrareze, Carlos Raimondi, Marcelo Mendes, Joaquim Silveira, Paulo Roberto Bertaglia, Greg Robins, Dennis Stolkey, Todd Taylor, and Judy Cole.

And I want to make a special acknowledgment to Orlando Pavani Jr., my master on human behavior, who not only helped me to understand others, but helped me to better understand myself first.

Lastly, I thank Steven Howard, my publishing partner and editor, who transformed my ideas and thoughts into this book. He has been a wonderful mentor throughout this process, crafting words into what we hope will be a legacy product for our readers.

About the Author

"I can accept failure.
Everyone fails at something.
But I can't accept not trying."
MICHAEL JORDAN

Rodrigo S. Martineli was born in 1980 in the city of Santo André, São Paulo state in Brazil.

His childhood was split living in São Caetano do Sul, part of São Paulo metroplex, Belém, north of Brazil and São José do Rio Preto, in the countryside of São Paulo state.

He started his professional and entrepreneurial career when he was 14 years old, selling business cards to stores in Brazil. After five years of building his own business, in addition to working as a salesman for a clothing store, he started his corporate career as an intern.

In a matter of four years, he was expatriated to Mexico to lead an operation as his first managerial experience. Right after that, he moved to Buenos Aires, Argentina. By the time he was 24 years old, he was responsible for global operations in 19 countries overseeing around 200 people across Latin America.

In 2006, he married Carolina, and that's when their first baby, a French bulldog named Nicole, joined the family. In 2009, the family got bigger and Apollo, another French bulldog, joined them.

During these career years, he worked in many different roles: Project & Program Management, Business Manager, Strategy & Sales Leader.

The family started to get complete when the first boy of the family, Felipe, was born in 2013.

In late 2013, he reached a true Global Executive status, leading a multi-billion-dollar business. This required relocating to Frisco, Texas, and leaving his parents, big brother, and little sister in Brazil.

In 2015 the second boy of the family, the Texan Thomas, was born, completing the family.

Rodrigo loves to work and dedicates time to his family, travel, and sports. A die-hard New England Patriots fan and a passionate fan of the Dallas Mavericks, you usually see him attending their home games. He also loves to spend time playing tennis, golf, and, believe it or not, video games.

He is an accomplished senior executive with well-rounded experience built during a corporate career that started in 1999, working in Fortune 100 companies and growing billion-dollar enterprises.

He is a genuine general manager with expertise in business development, delivering consistent top and bottom-line growth where he usually led exponential business growth.

With his strong executive presence, business acumen, and global and cultural experience, he has built businesses to strive for the best using his simple but effective methodologies to assure a faster, more consistent execution.

Education
He has a degree in Business Management and Executive Education from Harvard Business School (HBS) in Emerging Markets, and Corporate Governance from Kellogg School of Management (Northwestern University). In addition, several human development, human behavior, and neuroscience courses complement his skills.

In March 2017, he was granted a Declaration of Human Behavior Improvement (DHBI) certification endorsing his ability to better understand himself and others by deploying multi-behavioral techniques in the pursuit of human peak performance.

He speaks Portuguese (natively), English, and Spanish.

Feel free to connect or follow him on LinkedIn at www.linkedin.com/in/rodrigomartineli/

Printed in the USA
CPSIA information can be obtained
at www.ICGtesting.com
LVHW012119210124
769368LV00002B/129